# SUCCESSFUL RECOVERY AND RELAPSE PREVENTION

# SUCCESSFUL RECOVERY
# AND RELAPSE PREVENTION

Bill McCausland Ph.D.

# SUCCESSFUL RECOVERY GROUP

## Understanding Recovery and Relapse Prevention

**Orientation and Summary Points.** Welcome to the Successful Recovery Group. The purpose of this section is to have you think about what you need for your personal recovery plan, to understand the levels of recovery, to realize how the compulsion to use changes with time in recovery, to be familiar with relapse myths, and to determine if there is a difference between a slip and a relapse.

A.  What are your goals to make your recovery happen for you?

- What will it take for you to be clean and sober?

- Where do you want to be?

- What will it take to get you there?

B.  Three levels of recovery:

- Physical recovery

- Thinking recovery

- Feeling recovery

C.  Phases of recovery:

- I can't use.

- I won't use.

- I don't use.

D.  Relapse Myths:

- Myth #1: Relapse is inevitable.

- Myth #2: Relapse inevitably means failure.

- Myth #3: Relapse can't be prevented.

- Myth #4: Relapse after a period of sobriety, and it will take months or years to hit bottom again

E.  Is there a difference between a slip versus a relapse?

**A. Goals for the Successful Recovery Educational Group**. The following goals for recovery and preventing relapse are recommended to help you learn more about addiction and to help you take responsibility for recovery.

1. **Don't use mood-altering substances.** Any substance use can trigger a relapse and prevent you from engaging in practices that promote recovery.

2. **Understand the illness of addiction.** The idea of the "disease concept of addiction" is an essential guiding force in understanding the effects that addiction has on you and will help you begin to identify what you need to do in the process of recovery. Learning that you need to manage the disease and that you can't cure it is a major concept that will help you change.

3. **Develop a state of mind and choose behaviors that keep you alcohol and drug-free.** Learn that how you think, how you feel, and what you do drive whether you stay clean and sober or go back to substance use. Recovery is a state of mind and an acceptance of the fact that you are chemically dependent.

4. **Develop a daily and weekly recovery plan.** There needs to be a plan to make recovery happen. Good recovery requires good planning.

5. **Start identifying warning signs of relapse and triggers and have a plan to deal with them.** The group will help you start to have more awareness of various warning signs and help you begin to identify those that are particularly relevant to you. You will develop a plan to handle to warning signs based on the new information you are learning.

6. **Recovery: an active process of personal growth.** Recovery is an active process, and it is powerful to hear people say, "I'm working a program." Passivity leads to relapse since there is a natural tendency to revert to old ways unless you are actively working a program of recovery.

Have you heard the term, "grateful alcoholic" or "grateful addict"? What is that? It means that recovery is more than not using alcohol and drugs. Recovery gives you your life back. One meaning of being grateful in recovery is that you gain access to your many potentials as a human being; you have an understanding of things that nonrecovering people do not have.

Step One of the Twelve Steps says that "our lives had become unmanageable." Recovery is understanding what unmanageability means for you. For some, life seems unmanageable in addition to the unmanageability directly caused by substance use. Recovery is actively working on resolving the unmanageable aspects of your life, whether they are related or not related to substance abuse.

7. **Understanding phases of recovery.** Recovery has stages, and it is a developmental process where you move from one stage to the next. You will learn about the various issues that come up in each stage of recovery.

8. **Develop your healthy coping mechanisms to maintain sobriety.** Do everything you can in recovery to develop healthy coping mechanisms. Nothing is too small.

9. Learn the nature of addiction and recovery.

10. Understand it.

11. Apply recovery to you.

12. Find specific techniques for taking care of yourself

B. **Three levels of recovery.** Working on the following levels of recovery is an ongoing process where the goal is progress. Recovery has several dimensions in addition to abstinence, or "putting the plug in the jug." Some people can be abstinent for a period of time but will return to using alcohol or drugs, since other elements have to be taken care of to be truly sober. Only putting the plug in the jug isn't enough because recovery is a three-part process:

> - Physical Recovery
> - Thinking Recovery
> - Feeling Recovery

1. **Physical Recovery.** You can't be in recovery if you are using any mood-altering substance.

- Abstinence from all mood-altering substances is important. Know what is mood-altering (see the appendix in the workbook to reference abusable drugs).

- Know safe use of prescription medication.

- Don't switch addictions.

- Watch out for compulsive behaviors that change the way you feel, such as gambling, shopping, eating, sex, etc.

The definition of physical abstinence is not taking any abusable substances into your body. Physical recovery is also allowing your body to heal from the effects of substance abuse and getting medical consultation if there is the possibility of damage caused by your use of alcohol or drugs. Physical recovery is understanding that your brain needs to heal from the effects of substance use.

Physical recovery in the initial stage of abstinence happens by giving yourself time to go through the withdrawal period, which might be marked by symptoms of insomnia (caffeine use can exacerbate insomnia), depression, anxiety, and other forms of distress. Your body needs to recover, and most people feel a lot of improvement of these symptoms within a month. Working on having a supernutritious diet, good hydration with nonsugary liquids, enough sleep and rest, and exercise are major actions to help your physical recovery. What other self-care measures do you need to do? At the end of this section, there is a place for you to write down what your body needs to heal and what self-care you need to do for recovery.

Know what substances are mood-altering. Physical recovery is knowing what prescription drugs are abusable and taking personal responsibility for advising your health-care providers (MD, nurse practitioner, dentist, etc.) that you are a person in recovery. There needs to be a solid plan if an abusable drug is going to be prescribed. Unfortunately, a lot of providers do not fully understand addiction and that a single use of an abusable drug can trigger a chain reaction and relapse, regardless of whether it was your drug of choice or not. Discuss any issues with your recovery staff or recovery addiction medicine physician.

Physical recovery is making sure you do not deceive yourself into using a mood-altering substance other than your drug of choice. Sometimes people compulsively use caffeine, and this can lead to relapse. There are also other behaviors that can be done compulsively which are escapist and give an adrenaline rush. They can be done compulsively to change the way you feel. Examples of these behaviors are gambling, shopping, eating, sex, etc.

2. **Thinking Recovery.** Self-honesty, reality-based thoughts, honesty with others.

   - Self-honesty vs. self-deception

   - Denial vs. reality

- Impaired thinking vs. being truthful with yourself

- Manipulating others vs. being honest

Thinking recovery is being reality-based and truthful with yourself. For most alcoholics and drug addicts, self-deception goes hand-in-hand with addiction. How else could you ignore the impact that alcohol or drugs were having on your life?

> You may find some perspective by knowing that alcoholics and drug addicts typically use denial unconsciously and automatically.

> Denial is usually not done on purpose, and it is part of addictive illness.

Denial is a term that covers a wide repertoire of psychological defenses that protects you from the realization that you are chemically dependent. It is important to know that alcoholics and drug addicts usually use denial unconsciously and automatically. It is typically not done on purpose. Examples are rationalization, which is an excuse or justification; blame, which is a means of deflection and puts responsibility onto someone or something else; minimizing, thinking "it isn't that big of a deal," etc. (Please see the next section, building up to relapse, for more on denial.)

Impaired thinking is related to denial. Having impaired thoughts allow you to not think of yourself as an alcoholic or a drug addict. "I am not an alcoholic or drug addict because . . . I'm too young. I'm too smart. I'm responsible at work. I never drink before five o'clock. I only use pot. My friend is an addict, now that's an addict, ad nauseam.

Another piece of alcoholic or drug-addict thinking may be the distortion of reality for the purpose of manipulating others around you. Basically, this is manipulating others into getting your way, especially making some rationalization or justification so you can use alcohol or drugs. Having an alibi for your spouse is an example. Usually, these manipulations make family members question their own reality; they can be "crazy making." Another distortion is manipulating a doctor to get a drug you want or, "lying by omission."

Thinking recovery is living life on life's terms and accepting reality for what it is. Many people in recovery used various forms of denial so much when they were using alcohol or drugs that it became a pattern in their lives, to the degree that it became an automatic response. These patterns have the tendency of carrying through into recovery. How to deal with them? Get feedback from others. Attend a lot of groups that are specifically related to recovery. Be in touch with that part of yourself that has self-honesty and is wise.

3.  **Feeling Recovery.** Emotional maturity.

- Learn to identify and cope with feelings in healthy ways.

- Early recovery can equal feeling a lot and feeling overwhelmed.

- Did your emotional development stop when you started using alcohol or drugs? You may feel that you are back to feeling as awkward as a teenager, which is when most people started using or drinking and when there was a lot to learn about yourself.

Change one thing: Stop using alcohol and drugs and check out the feelings that emerge. At times, this can be overwhelming for a lot of people in early recovery. The best part is that you are not alone and people in group and twelve-step meetings have some idea of what you are going through. Talk about how you feel instead of being isolated. One might say, "I am angry because I can't do my thing with boozing and using." There is a flip side to everything—you can have life another way, a way where you take the authority back that you gave over to alcohol or drugs, and you can change your anger into gratitude.

What are the strides with emotional maturity that people can make in recovery? The examples of changes seem endless, but here are a few:

## EMOTIONAL IMMATURITY

Having excessive false pride—being so thin-skinned that you have trouble admitting human weakness

Having perfectionism and unrealistic standards

## EMOTIONAL MATURITY

Admitting powerlessness and unmanageability and realizing that being humble does not mean being weak

Accepting yourself and your human mistakes, as well as the mistakes of others, and having realistic standards

| | |
|---|---|
| Being phony: having to look good to others | Being yourself and giving yourself credit |
| Selfishness: "I want what I want when I want it." | Sharing: When you start to feel good about yourself, you begin to care about the welfare and happiness of others. |
| Impatience | Patience |
| Self-pity | Finding reasons to feel worthwhile and good about yourself. If you want to have good self-esteem, do esteemable things; do the right thing. |
| Resentment (Latin base, meaning to "re-feel") | Forgiveness, understanding, and letting go |
| Staying intolerant and being judgmental | Developing tolerance |
| Procrastination | Getting the job done |
| Feeling guilt and shame | Letting go of guilt and shame and stopping self-hate |
| Fear and anxiety (expecting a catastrophe, or fearing someone will discover your flaws, or being anxious that you will get rejected, or imagining what will happen in the future and attaching various fears to it) | Acceptance of the world around us and living in the present. |
| Looking at the negative, at what is wrong | Gratitude and accentuating the positive |
| Avoiding conflicts within yourself and with others | Facing issues and resolving them or developing a plan for resolution |
| Hanging onto ill feelings and resentments | The willingness to let go |

Sometimes twelve-step sponsors will address some of the above emotional maturity issues in the Fourth Step, but you can start thinking about it now and begin applying the principles.

How is your emotional development? Some feel that their emotional development stopped or was significantly compromised when they started to use alcohol or drugs, "I am forty-five years old, and I feel like I cope with things like a teenager." Do you feel like your ability to cope seems broken, or maybe you wish that someone had taught you better ways of coping when you were growing up? One answer is to live for today, one day at a time, doing your best to cope with life on a daily basis, listening and talking to others, and seeking opportunities to gain skills to manage your feelings. Eventually, and over time, you will have progress.

Gaining skills for coping with feelings that come up on a daily basis in early recovery—depression, anxiety, distress tolerance, boredom, elation, and so on—will be a topic in your recovery skill class. Tune in.

C. **Phases of Compulsion to Use Alcohol or Drugs.** Your compulsion to use alcohol or drugs will change over time. The change will have to do with your acceptance of your need to be in recovery and having the intrinsic motivation to get clean and sober, that is, doing it for one primary person— yourself. The second reason: Your attitude will change as a result of allowing enough time for your brain to heal from the effects of substance abuse.

> - I can't
>
> - I won't
>
> - I don't

1. **I Can't.** The realization of problems with substance abuse, which motivates you to stop using alcohol or drugs.

   - Realization that you can't safely use alcohol or drugs

   - External pressure caused by consequences

   - External pressure not to use initially helps motivate you for treatment but will not sustain you over the long haul because you ultimately have to do it for yourself

> ➤ The realization: Consequences tell me it's not safe.
>
> ➤ External pressures tell me, "Stop it."

You have the realization that you can't safely use alcohol or drugs. This hard fact comes through consequences of your use. You know somewhere in your mind that you need to stop using. There is probably some sort of external pressure to stop using alcohol or drugs and to get some help—for example, pressure from your spouse, employer, a health problem, a legal problem, and so on. This realization and pressure usually provides an external motivation for getting you to stop using alcohol or drugs and get help. But it will not provide the motivation that is necessary to sustain you over the long haul for getting clean and sober. Getting sober because it is a good idea, or for someone else, is not enough. It may help start your recovery, but it won't work as the only reason to get sober and stay sober.

2. **I Won't.** Making the shift of not wanting to use but still feeling some compulsion.

- Shift to an internal motivation for recovery

- The foot and a half drop

- Getting sober for yourself

- May still feel some compulsion to use

> ➤ The foot and a half drop—from my head to my heart.
>
> ➤ Getting sober for myself and not somebody else.

Some people in recovery call the shift to this phase as the "foot and a half drop." This is because there is a shift from knowing in your head to feeling in your heart that you want to be clean and sober. It is about becoming internally motivated to be in sobriety. You may feel some compulsion to use alcohol or drugs, but you're not sitting on the fence about whether to be in recovery. You start to get and feel some of the benefits of recovery, such as starting to feel significantly better about yourself, having new sober friends in recovery, and starting to see that "I can really do this." You might even feel some elation which some call the "pink cloud." There is more to come because the pink cloud doesn't last forever.

3. **I don't.** Feeling more of a personal identity of being in recovery.

- Identify with recovery

- Principles of recovery are integrated

- Using not an option

- More comfortable in recovery

- Compulsion to use is mostly gone

➢ Life is more balanced

This phase of recovery is about feeling more serenity and having a sense of freedom as a result of being vigilant about recovery. Applying the principles of recovery is the option for living life, as opposed to using alcohol or drugs to cope with life. In this phase, we become more accepting of ourselves as human beings, along with our imperfections. There is more humility. A lot of people in this phase find it helpful to do an inventory to assess on a daily basis the existence of selfishness, dishonesty, resentment, or fear and take some corrective action. Life is experienced in a more balanced way. The compulsion to use is replaced by principles of recovery.

**D. Myths Related to Relapse:** (Adapted from Dr. Al Mooney's *The Recovery Book*. This book is recommended and is a concise encyclopedia-like resource.) Relapse myths have grown into existence as a result of relapse being so shrouded in shame, guilt, anxiety, and misperception. Myths should be recognized because they can have a dangerous impact on how you think about sobriety and how you practice recovery.

**Myth #1: "Relapse is inevitable."** You might think that relapse is part of recovery because it is so talked about. True, relapse can be one symptom of the disease of addiction, but in no way is it a requirement in the process of recovery. One reason to dispel this myth is because if you believe relapse is inevitable, you may give yourself permission to use during rough times. Instead, give yourself the opportunity to successfully navigate the difficult moments so your recovery can be stronger as a result of you not relapsing.

One form of crazy thinking is "I might as well slip and get it over with so I can get on with my recovery." The fact is that people do not have to relapse in the process of recovery. Instead, wait for the compulsion to pass if you feel the urge to use; do the behaviors that support your recovery and get insight to deepen your understanding about yourself as a recovering person.

**Myth #2: "Relapse inevitably means failure."** Relapsing because of a lack of understanding the power of addictive illness or not being ready for recovery doesn't mean you can't get it the next time around. Relapse should only represent a false start and not exclude you from getting sober. Learn from it, move on, and get clean and sober—then relapse doesn't equal failure.

Relapse usually means that you were unsuspecting about the underlying trickery and forcefulness of addiction, in denial of what you need to do in the process of recovery, missing something essential to stay sober, having overconfidence, or feeling lazy and thinking you could get away with "half measures" to get sober (see below for a description of half measures). Relapse might reflect not being fully committed to sobriety or that you may have not felt enough pain to convince yourself that you can't safely use again. You may have not been motivated enough to develop the tools to stay sober. You have to learn, learn, learn if a relapse happens; otherwise the causes will repeatedly threaten your ability to recover.

**Myth #3: "Relapse can't be prevented."** Relapse is totally avoidable. Preventing it is about truly understanding addictive disease and the causes of relapse. The more knowledgeable you are about how to minimize the risks and knowing relapse warning signs will help you to know what recovery skills to be practicing, especially if you feel in danger of relapse.

**Myth #4: "Relapse after a period of sobriety, and it will take months or years to hit bottom again."** Addictive disease is progressive and irreversible (see "The Disease Concept of Addiction" in Section 5 of the workbook). This means that the disease gets worse—not better. Consequently, you will probably return to where you left off when you got sober and then relapsed. Addiction can also become worse during times of abstinence because of "shadow progression," the phenomenon which occurs when the disease of addiction progresses despite not using any alcohol or drugs. You may find that the addiction can actually be worse than where you left off if you go back to using after a period of sobriety. Because of progression and irreversibility, people who relapse usually hit bottom very soon, if not right away.

E. **Various Nonrecovery States: Slips and Relapses.** Do you think there is a distinction between a slip and a relapse? Some people who are trying to get sober fall into a lapse, pick themselves up, dust themselves off, and get back into recovery. This might be called a slip. Other people feel that any use of alcohol or drugs is a relapse.

**Taking breaks vs. actually being in recovery.** Some people seek treatment but haven't really made the decision to get sober. You might want to get sober, but there is no commitment to do what it actually takes to be sober. You might just want to get someone off your back so you seek treatment, but the idea in the back of your mind is to use at some later time. There may be the secret thought: "I'm going to keep my options open" or "I don't want to be without an escape hatch." Then there may be a periodic using episode and you call it a "slip." Maybe there are multiple slips. Let's call this scenario "taking a break" because you are stopping use for a period, but there is the conscious or unconscious plan to use periodically or in the future.

There are some people who try to customize their recovery programs to suit their needs—"an easier, softer way"—then relapse. Then there may be the realization, "Oops, that didn't work too well. What do I really need to do to get sober?" Try listening to what others have to say and getting humble.

An example of customizing a program of recovery would be what is called "half measures." Your sponsor or the treatment program recommends attending a certain number of meetings, or various types of reading, or writing on a first step, and you think, "This is too much work. I feel pretty good, and I don't need to go through all this stuff to get sober. I can do it my way, and that's all I need to do." Different forms of resistance may come up, and it is natural, but work on willingness, openness, and being teachable. It is a mistake to underestimate the power of addictive illness.

A major danger for alcoholics and drug addicts is that the brain has been reconditioned by the abuse of alcohol or drugs, and any use of any substance can set off a chain reaction of compulsive substance use.

> *Any use can set off a chain reaction.*

What do you think is the difference, if any, between a slip and a relapse? Most people in recovery consider any use of alcohol or drugs to be a relapse. Any use requires you to change your sobriety date.

| SLIP | RELAPSE |
|---|---|
| The recovering person promptly and freely admits to having a "slip" | Is dishonest, lies |
| Seeks help within twenty-four hours | Refuses help |
| Recovering person continues in recovery program | Stops going to meetings or goes intoxicated; stops seeing sponsor, recovery friends, etc. |
| No more than one previous slip | Multiple relapses |
| Takes a twenty-four-hour chip at twelve-step meeting | Withdraws, disappears, disappoints |
| Sponsor and significant others are informed, and support is continued for recovery | Family, friends, support abandoned |
| No severe, adverse consequences of family, work, legal, health, or social elements | Adverse life consequences |
| Recovering person agrees to new stringent recovery contact | Breaks recovery contract |

**What do you think is the difference, if any, between a slip and a relapse?**

Slip:_____

_____

_____

_____

Relapse:_____

_____

_____

_____

**Do you think that there is actually a difference between a slip and a relapse? Why?**

_____

_____

_____

_____

**Personal examples—of your own or others:**_____

_____

_____

_____

_____

_____

_____

_____

**What will it take for you to be clean and sober?**

**Where do you want to be?**

- _____

- _____

- _____

- _____

- _____

- _____

- _____

- _____

**What will it take?**

- _____

- _____

- _____

- _____

- _____

- _____

- _____

- _____

**What do you need to do to let your body heal?**

**What self-care do you need to do for recovery?**

_____

_____

_____

_____

_____

_____

_____

_____

# References

Mooney, A., Eisenberg, A., Eisenberg, H. (1992). The Recovery Book. New York: Workman Publishing Company, Inc.

Presti, D. (2006). Neurobiology of Addiction. California Society of Addiction Medicine Review Course 2006.

Step Four: Knowing Yourself (1993). In: The twelve steps of alcoholics anonymous: interpreted by the Hazelden Foundation. Center City, MI: Hazelden Foundation.

Talbott, D. (1995). Haight-Ashbury Conference, breakout provided by Douglas Talbott, M.D. of Talbott Recovery Systems, Atlanta Georgia.

Zimberg, S. (1987). Principles of alcoholism psychotherapy. In: S. Zimbert, J. Wallace & S.B. Blume (eds.). New York: Plenum Press.

# SUCCESSFUL RECOVERY GROUP

## Building Up to Relapse
## versus Maintaining Recovery

**Orientation and Summary Points.** The purpose of this section is for learning and increasing awareness about how the process of relapse occurs over time.

**A.** *Relapse is a process that builds up over time.*

**B.** *What is linked to relapse?*

- ✓ Losing the decision to be sober.

- ✓ Losing contact with your recovery support system.

- ✓ Not having enough coping mechanisms.

**C.** *Sequence of relapse: The Domino Effect*

1. Perceived control after having time in abstinence

2. Limited ability to cope and resorting to denial

3. Being in a high-risk situation

4. Being vulnerable to use

5. Thinking of using as a possibility

6. Attempted use

7. Violation of sobriety effect: "I already blew it, so I might as well use some more."

8. Feel shame, guilt, and loss of control

9. Reject the identity of being abstinent

**D.** *Do your relapse autopsy.* Analyze the buildup process if you were in recovery in the past and relapsed. Anticipate how you would build up to relapse if this is your first time in recovery. What do you need to do to maintain recovery?

A. **Relapse is a process.** Addiction does not go away. The part of addiction that has to do with the actual use of alcohol or drugs is asleep when you are abstinent. Some people say, "It is outside in the parking lot, doing push-ups." This means that addiction can gain strength during abstinence and it lies in wait to be awakened. It also implies that it is easy to get lulled into a false sense of security when you are abstinent and easy to underestimate the power of addiction. So addiction is like an organism that lives within us, but we are not victims to it as long as we are actively in recovery.

Relapse is a process, meaning there is a systematic series of events that occur which can lead to losing your sobriety. This sequence typically happens in the absence of a strong enough recovery program and in the absence of practicing the principles of recovery. As the saying in AA goes, "Half measures availed us nothing," and "Be willing to go to any lengths (for recovery)."

1. **Avoid being snagged by a relapse process, one day at a time.** Work on sobriety daily. We can plan and take steps for tomorrow, but it is only possible to take responsibility for what happens today. The one day at a time approach also means it is important to take life in doable chunks and not to get anxious and overwhelmed thinking about future events that you have no control over anyway. One day at a time means to have focus on recovery each day and to have the recovery state of mind each day because the seeds of relapse can be sown today and end growing up into a disaster later. In contrast, the seeds sown today for recovery can bring sobriety tomorrow. These two possible tracks demonstrate why it is important to go to meetings and do other things for your recovery even if you don't feel like it on a particular day.

> One day at a time. Take responsibility of recovery for today. You don't have control over tomorrow. What you do today sows the seeds for tomorrow, whether that is to maintain sobriety or to go back to using.

You may have heard the saying, "The person who has the most sobriety is the one that got up the earliest today." This means that recovery has a one-day-at-a-time focus, regardless of whether a person has one week or thirty years of sobriety.

2. **Relapse occurs over time.** Relapse typically occurs over time. It develops as a small groundswell and builds up to a huge wave that comes crashing down on the shore. A relapse can start with a seemingly small stressor or issue, the impact of which is either denied or avoided: "It's not that big of a deal," "I'll take care of it later," "I don't want to

deal with that situation because it is too tough." When this happens, other stressors or problems can accumulate in what seems like a relapse magnet that can culminate in losing sobriety.

There is also what might be called a theory of catastrophe, which means that failing to do small things for your recovery (going to meetings, calling people in the fellowship, contacting your sponsor, etc.) can lead to dramatic consequences with unpredictable timing and magnitude. Two or more small things can line up at one time to unhinge you.

Sabotaging yourself may also occur by finding some issue to make a big deal over, then letting it erode your sobriety. This might be the creation of a problem where a problem does not have to exist.

3.  **Recovery is dynamic.** Recovery is a fairly active process, and the more you practice it, the stronger it gets. It is like lifting weights to get strong muscles.

Using alcohol or drugs gets to feel normal with long-term use. It almost feels abnormal when you stop using and during the stages of early recovery. The drug or alcohol use that feels normal to the alcoholic or drug addict appears to be totally crazy to nonalcoholics or non–drug addicts: "Why doesn't she just stop?" "Why don't you control it and stop causing so much trouble?" During later stages of recovery, your set point changes and the idea of using alcohol or drugs no longer feels normal: "I don't feel like I want or have to use."

Consequently, if you don't stay engaged in your recovery program, you are most likely to revert back to what is normal for the alcoholic or drug addict—using alcohol or drugs. Using is a default position without active participation in recovery. Passivity increases the likelihood of regressing back to old patterns of behavior that are associated with using alcohol or drugs. You may not cope with life on life's terms and may start slipping into ways of coping via denial, manipulation, and dishonesty. You have two choices—either you are working on recovery or you are working on a relapse.

---

Either you are working on recovery or you are working on a relapse.

---

**Some Symptoms Linked to Relapse**

1. **Losing the decision to be clean and sober.** A crisis may have motivated you to get into recovery; the crisis passes, and so does your motivation. Complacency about working a recovery program is linked to decision loss.

2. **Losing contact with people that support your recovery program.** Recovery requires support. Losing contact may also lead to isolation, which can subsequently lead to relapse.

3. **Not having enough coping mechanisms.** This occurs when your problems and stresses overwhelm your ability to deal with them.

    • Especially when there is a "catastrophe," where several things have built up and converged all at once

    • Multiple stressors build up over time and create a critical mass

B. **The domino effect: Sequence of relapse process.** Everyone has symptoms and warning signs of relapse from time to time. This is not necessarily a big deal. The grist for the mill for recovery is the ability to recognize the warning symptoms of relapse and to deal with them. It is crucial to be open to feedback from others when you might be in a relapse process. We all have blind spots (areas where we lack awareness). Part of recovery is wanting feedback from others and actually listening to it in order to help identify and deal with blind spots.

There are variations of the relapse process, and the following is a general pattern:

1. **Perceived control.** You might start feeling that you have control during periods of abstinence, and this feeling of control may increase over time. Perhaps the stresses that occurred due to the consequences of your drug or alcohol use have died down. You might also start feeling like a "normal person." There may be less of a motivation to be engaged in an active program of recovery. The central issue is that you forget the powerlessness against and unmanageability of addictive illness.

> Forgetting the powerlessness against
> and unmanageability of addictive illness—not a good idea!

You might start to feel more complacent about recovery and start to skip going to meetings, contacting your sponsor, or being around other people who support your recovery. You might start to feel like you can handle being around alcohol or drugs or being in situations which in the past were associated with using alcohol or drugs. Another example is being out of your "comfort zone" with no plan to take care of your sobriety, thinking that you are in control enough to handle a vacation, business trip, holiday, party, wedding, and so on, without enough consideration of how sobriety is going to fit into the mix.

2. **Limited ability to cope—resorting to denial.** The use of alcohol or drugs creates an enormous, but faulty, way to cope with life. In the end, it is a flawed and maladaptive way to deal with problems and stress because it actually creates more problems and stresses due to the consequences of use. There is momentary relief, but the payback is with a lot of interest. Part of the disease of addiction is thinking that using is a viable way to cope.

Being in recovery provides endless possibilities for coping with day-to-day problems and stress, but you need to actually be in recovery in order to engage in more effectively. As the domino effect proceeds, you may feel that you are in control, but you may not be likely to use recovery mechanisms and support to cope. A lot of people with alcohol and drug problems do not have very good ways of coping with problems and stress, and when things build up, they may feel overwhelmed. Because the alcoholic or addict may have a "broken coper" or have never learned to deal with problems in the first place, the default position may be to become defensive in some way. Feeling defensive creates denial.

*Denial*: a general term to describe many defenses and maneuvers that are unconsciously and automatically set up in order to protect the person from the conflict of being chemically dependent. It is part of addictive illness because it serves to protect the addiction by not allowing the person to sufficiently realize that he or she is chemically dependent. Denial is all about self-deception and distorted reality. It may come in the form of denying to some degree the existence of addiction or denying the consequences caused by the addiction. Examples of denial are simple denial ("I don't have a problem"), minimizing, rationalization, justification, and so on.

> *Denial ain't just a river in Egypt.*
>
> —Mark Twain
> (1835–1910)

Denial is used as a maneuver to get people off your back so you can continue to use alcohol or drugs. This is a form of dishonesty that is used to manipulate people. It is all about deception and selling a version of distorted reality to someone else. You may have heard the saying: "The perfect manipulation is the manipulation that goes unnoticed." This means that when you are manipulating someone, they don't realize it, and this creates a perfect agenda to keep on doing your thing with alcohol or drugs.

Maneuvering people is about control. You feel out of control on the inside and want to use alcohol or drugs, and you compensate by controlling others so you can use. Examples are having alibis, blaming, half-truths, lying by omission, using anger to control others, giving a particular spin on reality to get what you want, and so on.

A lot of the time people who live with an alcoholic or a drug addict feel somewhat crazy because perception of reality gets distorted by the substance abuser; the sense of reality gets strained. Part of the family disease of addiction is the family also denies in some way that the alcoholic or drug addict is addicted, like the story of the elephant in the room—there is an elephant in the living room, and nobody talks about it.

Distress builds up over time if the denial and maneuvers are used to cope instead of using recovery-related and healthy ways of coping. The reason is that nothing ever get really gets resolved when there are defensive ways of trying to deal with problems and stresses. The opposite and healthy side of this is being reality-based, which is accurately evaluating a problem, finding a healthy solution, and doing it.

3.  **High-risk situations.** A high-risk situation is any circumstance that threatens your sobriety. There are seemingly countless variations on high-risk situations that can be a danger to recovery, but the following account for about two-thirds of high-risk situations that happen as part of the domino effect of relapse:

    1.  **Negative emotions:** Frustration, anger, depression, fear, anxiety, boredom, sleep deprivation, sensitivity concerning rejection, crisis, stress, hopelessness, and so on. In terms of gender, on average, anger tends to be more of a problem for men and depression more of a problem for women.

    2.  **Conflict with someone:** This could be an ongoing conflict or conflict that just happened in a relationship . . . marriage, family, friendship, work-related, etc. The conflict could be an overt argument or something you have suppressed and allowed to churn up inside you. Sometimes people set up conflicts with others, then have a justification for relapsing, and blame the other

person for the relapse: "I drank because of all the pressure that you put on me. It is your fault."

3.  **Social pressure:** A response to pressure, whether it is direct or indirect pressure to use alcohol or drugs.

*Direct social pressure* is being offered something to use: "You have been sober for six months now, and you can have one beer, can't you?" Old using friends may overtly or unwittingly sabotage your recovery by offering you alcohol or drugs. This might happen because they can't adjust to your recovery, make room for it, or they are naive, or feel threatened by it in some way.

*Indirect social pressure* is being around alcohol or drugs and feeling stimulated or triggered to use though no one is offering you anything.

4.  **Being vulnerable and in denial.** In the relapse process, there is perceived control, resorting to denial (because of not using healthy coping measures), and then there is encountering a high-risk situation. This series is like two setups and then the spike in a volleyball game. You are vulnerable, but may not totally realize it. The vulnerability could include not talking about your feelings, isolating yourself, or feeling isolated.

5.  **The possibility of using alcohol or drugs becomes an option.** You may automatically start thinking about using to get relief, get high, or to reach for something outside yourself to feel differently. There might being the feeling of wanting to escape.

    *   Fantasize: go into almost a trancelike state thinking about using.

    *   Obsess or become preoccupied: using may dominate your mind.

    *   Euphoric recall: "romancing the bottle," or remembering the good parts about using but forgetting the negative consequences—like your last detox, DUI, argument, etc. This is compartmentalized thinking, which is a form of denial.

    *   Saying some version of "The heck with it."

6.  **Attempted initial use.** There is delusional thinking that you can use now without any consequences. "I have been sober for some time now. I can probably use normally now." "All those problems I had in the past were just a fluke." "I'll have just one."

"I'll use today and quit tomorrow." "My substance of choice is alcohol, and I've never had a problem with pot. I'm going to use some pot." "I'm anxious, so I'll going to the doctor and get a tranquilizer."

7. **"The violation of sobriety effect."** The dominos come tumbling down. The door closed to alcohol or drug use moves from being open for just a crack to the door being wide open. Once you have already blown your sobriety, you might think, "Well, I have to change my sobriety date anyway, so I might as well make it worth it." "I used yesterday and already blew it, so I might as well use today too, and then I quit tomorrow." "I used two days ago, so one more day won't hurt."

The violation of sobriety effect can also be linked to behaviors that are connected with your alcohol or drug use. For example, if compulsive gambling, compulsive shopping, or sexual addiction is linked to your alcohol or drug use: "I gambled, so I might as well have a drink." "I'm back into the sexual thing, so I might as well use some meth."

8. **Feeling shame, guilt, and loss of control.** Being in recovery in the past really messes up your mind for using in the present. That is because there is gap between what you know is the right thing and what you are actually doing. What you think, know, value, feel, and believe tells you, "I shouldn't be using," but you are doing it anyway. For some people, there is the return to denial; for others, there is sinking into self-loathing, feeling worthless, or feeling really bad about oneself. You may have heard the saying about the discrepancy between what you know about using versus what you are doing: "There is nothing worse than a head full of AA and a belly full of booze."

9. **Rejecting the image of seeing oneself as a person in recovery.** This is the stage of full relapse, where the identity of being a person in recovery is lost. It may not be lost forever, but the grasp on recovery seems elusive. There might be a feeling of resignation: "Can't I ever get it?"

C. **The relapse autopsy: Analyzing past relapse or the potential for a relapse in the future.**

**Relapsed before? What led up to it, and what was missing?**

_____

_____

_____

_____
_____
_____
_____
_____
_____
_____

**What do you need to do to maintain your sobriety?**

_____
_____
_____
_____
_____
_____
_____
_____

**Never relapsed before? Imagine what would lead up to relapse if it were to happen to you.**

_____
_____
_____
_____
_____
_____
_____

**What do you need to do to take care of your recovery so you do not relapse?**

_____

_____

_____

_____

_____

_____

_____

_____

# References

Marlatt, A (1982). Reprint provided by Dr. Marlatt. Relapse prevention: Self-control program for the treatment of addictive behaviors. In: R. Stuart (Ed.), Adherence, compliance and generalization in behavioral medicine. New York: Brunner/Mazel, Inc.

University of California, San Diego (1998). Course materials in preparation for APA College of Professional Psychology's examination for certification in the treatment of alcohol and other psychoactive use disorders.

# SUCCESSFUL RECOVERY

## Relapse Warning Signs

**Orientation and Summary Points.** The purpose of this chapter is to increase your awareness of the warning signs that lead to relapse. Have a plan to deal with them to prevent relapse. Every warning sign has a flip side, a lesson for recovery.

**Two Sections:**

*The Abbreviated Version.* A summary and an overview to know about relapse warning signs at a glance. Check the warning signs that might apply to you and read about them in the full version.

*The Full Version.* Gives the full text about warning signs.

Warning signs vs. triggers:

- Relapse evolves over time.
- Warning signs precede relapse.
- Avoidance or unawareness of warning signs precede relapse.
- Triggers are more acute situations.

Warning signs can be positive:

- Signal an undercurrent and potential for relapse
- Signal the need to do something different in recovery to stay sober
- Grow by coming to terms with warning signs when they come up and ultimately have a stronger recovery

Three major warning signs:

a) *Thinking.* Thinking that is self-deceptive, thinking that may not support recovery, bargaining with the addiction.

b) *Feeling.* How feelings are coped with that come up in recovery.

c) *Behavioral.* What you do to support recovery or behaviors that lead to relapse.

> It's a lot easier to stay sober than it is to relapse and get sober again!

## THINKING, FEELING AND BEHAVIORAL
## RELAPSE WARNING SIGNS
### The Abbreviated Version

A. **Thinking Warning Signs**

1. **Priority:** SLIP—Sobriety loses its priority

2. **Overconfidence:** "I'll never use again."

3. **Being judgmental:** Being critical of others in sobriety is a distance maker and a way of disidentifying with recovery.

4. **Stress:** Not realizing all the adjustments that are necessary in recovery

5. **Negative thinking:** Attracts more negative thinking

6. **Only one drink:** "Maybe I can use normally now."

7. **Thinking of using to cope:** "Using is the only way I can get through this."

8. **I don't care:** "Recovery isn't worth it."

9. **Thinking of using another drug:** Switching addictions or going back to your drug of choice

10. **I'm unique:** "I can do it my way, and you don't understand."

11. **Sabotage:** Shooting yourself in the foot with underlying low self-esteem

12. **Romancing the bottle:** Thinking of alcohol or drugs like your lost lover that you want to reconnect with

B. **Feeling Warning Signs**

1. **Difficulty managing:** Emotions and feeling are running you or acting on you

2. **Overwhelmed:** Everything happening all at once

3. **Shame and guilt:** You are your own worst critic; comes with regret

4. **Depression:** Caused by physical effects of substance use and consequences of use

5. **Hopelessness:** Accumulation of problems; recovery is too tough.

6. **Self-pity:** "Not going my way," no recognition, "I'm suffering, and nobody cares."

7. **Frustration and anger:** Blocked from what you want; a lot of frustration; addicted to rage; a setup to use

8. **Anxiety:** Scaring yourself

9. **Bored:** Not using substances has left a vacuum, and you don't know what to do.

10. **Resentment:** The Big Book says it's the "number one offender."

11. **Loneliness:** Need new friends in recovery; are you isolating?

12. **Unresolved stress:** Unfinished emotional business, posttraumatic stress disorder (PTSD)

13. **Feeling stuck:** Being stuck is sometimes a natural occurrence in recovery. What does it mean for you and what do you do?

## C. Behavioral Warning Signs

1. **Loss of constructive planning:** Losing or not having a recovery plan

2. **Relationships:** New romantic relationship; spouse still uses; enduring conflicts and codependent roles.

3. **Drama positive vs. negative:** Add positive drama to your recovery to make it richer; negative drama creates conflicts that undermine recovery

4. **Compulsive behaviors:** Food, sex, spending, caffeine, work, gambling, the Internet.

5. **Dishonesty:** Forgetting rigorous honesty, lying to yourself, manipulating

6. **Isolating vs. solitude:** Disengage, and the addict mind automatically emerges.

7. **Alienating people who can help you:** Avoiding honest feedback, becoming irritable and angry with them.

8. **Procrastination:** Avoidance of what you need to do that can lead to feeling overwhelmed or an absence of recovery activities that leads to relapse

9. **Secrets:** You are as sick as your secrets.

10. **Rejecting input:** Others might know more, or they be more objective. As the A.A. saying goes, "Contempt prior to investigation."

11. **Complacency:** Losing your recovery edge with more time in recovery

12. **Associating with people who use:** Being drawn to people or places where there is use

# RELAPSE WARNING SIGNS

## The Full Version

### Introduction

**Warning signs vs. triggers.** Warning signs: Relapse usually evolves over time, and there are typically signs along the trail to relapse which indicate that it will occur. In contrast, triggers are more acute and occur in the moment which ignites the drive to want to use. Know your warning signs, and know your triggers. This section of your workbook will discuss warning signs. Triggers will be covered in the Mindful Recovery class.

**Warning signs can be positive.** Warning signs are only signs. In no way do they indicate that a relapse will actually occur. What they do indicate is that some sort of change has to take place in recovery. The need to make changes is tough for a lot of alcoholics and drug addicts: "I hurt . . . but I don't want to change." Avoidance or the procrastination in dealing with warning signs is a key element of eventual relapse. You don't want to relapse? Don't avoid what you need to do. When a warning sign comes up, do the next right thing, not the next wrong thing. Your feeling of personal effectiveness will increase . . . and that is a good thing for recovery.

> When a warning sign comes up, do the next right thing, not the next wrong thing.

The other major concern is being aware of relapse warning signs in the first place. You might not see a warning sign that relapse might occur. This is reflected in the AA saying, "[The disease of addiction] is cunning, baffling, and powerful." This means that the addict mind seems to have infinite creativity in sabotaging you without you being aware of it. If there was a secret code book that had the absolute corner on the truth, it would probably say that one way out of this mess would be awareness, self-honesty, and positive action.

Warning signs reveal that something different needs to happen in your recovery. In the positive sense, they indicate that you need to make the shift from what you are presently doing, and making a shift could result in personal growth.

### Three Major Warning Signs

a)   **Thinking warning signs:** Beliefs that distort reality of what you need to do to stay sober or trying to bargain with addiction in an attempt to keep on using

b)   **Feeling warning signs:** Unawareness or avoidance of feelings

c) **Behavior warning signs:** What you do affects what will happen. Recovery behavior = sobriety.

Addict/alcohol behavior = relapse

A. **Thinking warning signs:** Problems with self-honesty and the thinking about your approach to recovery. The following are some examples of self-deceptive thoughts that rationalize the use of alcohol or drugs or compromise recovery in some way:

- Sobriety is boring.

- I'll never use again.

- I can do it myself.

- I'm not as bad as . . .

- I owe this one to me.

- My problems can't be solved.

- I wish I was happy.

- I don't care.

- If nobody else cares, why should I?

- Things have changed. (I can use now.)

- I can handle it (using alcohol or drugs).

- I can't do it (stay sober).

- Why try?

- They don't know what they are talking about.

- There has got to be a better way.

- I can't change the way I think.

- If I move, everything will change.

- I like my old friends (who use).

- I can do things differently (so I can gain control).

- Nobody knows how I feel.

- I feel hopeless.

1. **Priority.** SLIP is an acronym meaning, "sobriety loses its priority." Everybody has a lot of priorities: family, making a living, friends, religion, health, interests, sports, leisure activities, clubs, and the list goes on. Recovery has to be your number one priority if you want to stay clean and sober. This doesn't mean that you don't have other priorities; it only means that it has to be your first priority. Sometimes there are competing priorities that demand your attention and you have to make choices about what is the best thing to do at any particular point in time. But keep time available to focus on your recovery if you want to stay clean and sober. Think about the saying, "You will lose everything anyway that you put ahead of your recovery."

2. **Overconfidence.** "I'll never drink or use again." "I wouldn't take another drink now, even if you paid me." "I feel absolutely no compulsion to use." "Recovery is a piece of cake. Why does everybody make such a big deal about it?" Overconfidence is self-deceptive thinking that you have some control of addiction, and there is usually an element of grandiosity. Addictive disease is cunning, baffling, and powerful, and the best antidote for overconfidence is humility and living recovery for today, one day at a time. If you are overconfident, try doing a realistic appraisal of your addiction. Overconfidence is the denial or naiveté of what one needs to do in the process of recovery.

3. **Being judgmental.** Looking for an excuse to use, being judgmental of other people in recovery or of people who are trying to help you get sober. Being judgmental is a distance maker and a way of disidentifying with recovery.

   Basically, being judgmental is saying that someone is a fool in some way because of the way the person is. Evaluating a situation is different than being judgmental because evaluation is more objective and does not have a put-down quality to it. Having likes and dislikes are also different than being judgmental because they simply express preferences.

   Obviously, you don't have to like everyone you come in contact with just because they are in recovery. But try to identify with the sameness: addictive illness. People in recovery have different characteristics than you: richer, poorer, smarter, dumber, higher bottoms, lower bottoms, but one thing that is the same is the element of addiction: "Addiction is an equal opportunity disease." The saying in AA, "principles before personalities," means that you're are not going to like everyone, but the important thing is to practice the principles of recovery.

Work on not being judgmental if you encounter hypocrisy with some people who are in recovery. Hypocrisy exists everywhere in life, but it doesn't necessarily discount the good things that people are trying to do for themselves. The existence of hypocrisy is a comment on living in an imperfect world.

4. **Impact of stress.** Adjustment to recovery. Begin to think that recovery is full of good changes, but despite the changes being good, they do require a lot of adjustment. Adjustment causes stress because it is not what you are used to. How you think about the adjustments in recovery will influence whether it is good stress or negative stress for you. Good stress is the excitement of the positive things you experience and what will come (self-esteem, self-respect, new friends, optimism, the absence of pain).

   Negative stress is "Oh man, I have to do what? This makes me feel out of control, anxious, depressed, and overwhelmed." What is your thinking about the impact of the changes you are making in the process of getting sober? The positive spin that you put on it will drive your recovery to sobriety.

5. **Negative thinking versus positive thinking.** Negative thoughts breed other negative thoughts and attract negativity like a magnet. What is behind your negative thinking, and what do you need to do to turn it around? The opposite is true for positive thoughts, so accentuate the positive (see resentments below).

6. **"I'll do some social drinking," "I think that I am going to have one drink," or "I am going to use just this one time."** This is the denial of the fact that you do not have control or that you just do not care anymore. This could be a variation on thinking that you are cured. Remember the First Step: We admitted we were powerless over alcohol or drugs—that our lives had become unmanageable. Call someone in the program before you use to get some reality testing. Think of the AA saying, "One is too many, a thousand is not enough."

7. **Thinking of using to cope.** You have emotional pain, are stressed out, and don't know how to cope. Under pressure, you might revert to the default position of using alcohol or drugs to cope. You don't have to go it alone, so get some help. Buy some time: "This too shall pass." Carry a phone list and call people in the program. Get a lot of practice at calling people so when you are in a crisis, it will be easier to call. Call before you use alcohol or drugs, not afterward. Think of using

the skills of recovery that you are learning in the treatment program and through the twelve-step programs.

8.  **Thinking "I don't care."** The consequences of using don't seem as bad as what you are feeling at a particular time in recovery. Some version of "The heck with it." This is one of the more self-destructive versions of stinking thinking. What is causing the "I don't care" attitude? Have you been running yourself ragged, getting too overwhelmed, or don't place enough value in yourself? The good news is that we have the power to change how we think. Step back and get some perspective. Go to meetings, be around positive people in recovery—the "winners"—and be open to allowing your thinking to be influenced in a positive direction. Treat yourself and reward yourself without using alcohol or drugs.

9.  **Thinking it is okay to use another drug.** Using a drug that is not your drug of choice leads to switching addictions or leads you back to your drug of choice. "Using another drug is like switching seats on the *Titanic*." That is, use leads you downward. "My drug of choice is meth, and I am going to use pot because there aren't the disastrous effects with pot that there were with meth." Any drug use will circumvent your ability to engage in a program of recovery . . . because you are still using! Please remember that, in general, your brain has been conditioned to use any abusable substance in an addictive way, regardless of what your drug of choice is.

10. **Thinking that you are unique.** "I'm different. You don't understand me. I am not like everybody else, and I can do recovery my way. I can customize the program to make it work my way," denial or naiveté of what you need to do to stay sober, taking an "an easier, softer way." "Terminal uniqueness" means thinking that you are unique, which will culminate in you destroying yourself. Realize that you are powerless over alcohol and drugs but you are not powerless over what you need to do in the process of recovery. There is the concept of "willingness." Simply, willingness is the openness to suggestion by others who know about recovery and doing what it takes to get sober.

    Self-centeredness and narcissism can also be elements associated with the feeling that you are unique. These are very dangerous things in recovery because they rob you of the perspective of accurately knowing what you need for recovery. Humility and being teachable are the keys.

11. **Sabotage.** You have heard about burning bridges behind you, but sabotaging yourself is burning the bridge in front of you or burning

the one that you are walking across. What is your thinking that underlies your sabotage? Is it "I am so screwed up and I have messed up so much that I do not deserve to have things be okay"? Or do you have trouble tolerating things being okay because in some twisted way, it is more comfortable to have chaos in your life? You might sabotage yourself because things get to be a little too smooth in recovery and you seek some sort of drama. Be in recovery by allowing yourself to be tolerant, forgiving, accepting, and patient with yourself, and work on finding some serenity (see below, positive vs. negative drama).

Give yourself positive self-affirmations: "I'm a good person." Low self-esteem causes self-sabotage. Be active with your self-esteem: Perform acts that create high self-esteem, not low self-esteem. Everyone deserves to have a better life as a result of getting clean and sober, regardless of who you are, the experiences you've had, or your background.

> Be active with your self-esteem: Do acts that create
> high self-esteem, not low self-esteem.

12. **Romancing the bottle.** You may have heard this term, which means idealizing the alcohol or the drug like a lost lover with whom you want to reconnect with. In some sense, it is also like "euphoric recall," where you remember the good things about using and cancel out the bad things. It is almost like personifying the substance, making it like a person and engaging in a process of mutual seduction . . . maybe like your secret love affair. You might feel as if you are going into an automatic trancelike state when thinking about your alcohol or drug. Snap out of the trance by doing the "talking cure"—talk about it and remember the consequences of your alcohol or drug use.

B. **Feeling warning signs.** Stop using alcohol and drugs and you start to feel, "Man, this is real!" You detox, you get off alcohol and drugs, and then you have yourself and your feelings. Welcome to the real thing. For a lot of the people in early recovery, the real thing is hard to handle. The change from using to sobriety, and the adjustment, is a process fraught with all kinds of feelings and emotions. It is a wonder that anybody gets sober at all, but the wondrous thing is that people do get sober despite all of the emotional turmoil of early recovery. Hang in there, and don't give up just before the miracle of recovery begins to happen for you.

Feeling warning signs tell you that you need to take care of some business, get support, get help, or have patience for the feeling to pass. These actions lead to recovery. Unawareness, passivity, tuning it out, and avoidance are what lead to relapse.

1. **Difficulty managing emotions and feelings.** They seem to be acting on you or running you, and you may feel like you have a lot of noise in your system. Your brain is talking to you on automatic pilot, and it is not saying very nice things. You may have heard of this being called "the committee," which represents all the competing voices and conflicts in your mind. Get outside yourself to objectively evaluate and deal with the committee. Call someone. Work on resolving the different aspects of your conflict. Go to a meeting. Get some exercise. Do something to soothe yourself. Write something. Listen to some good music.

2. **Feeling overwhelmed.** This is the "my plate is too full" syndrome. You have too much going on all at once, like a war movie where all of the troops are coming over the hill and are just about to blast you. Let go, give it up, and prioritize. Think of the most important thing or feeling that you have to deal with, and have that as your starting point. Deal with things in very small increments. Think of what you have to do this minute, not the rest of your life.

3. **Guilt and shame.** The critic: Are you your own worst critic, and do you have a critical voice within you that reminds you of negative consequences of your using alcohol and drugs? Do you feel guilty because of using and its consequences, and do you go ten rounds in the ring, beating yourself up? Do you feel guilty and want to make up for lost time, other losses, and hurts caused by your using? Is patience a problem, and do you want to have everything be okay right now? That can get you feeling intense, overwhelmed, and uptight. Understanding the disease of addiction and the destructive consequences that goes along with addiction is a major help. Your piece in the process is taking responsibility for yourself today and planning the remedies that will help you heal.

Shame is also driven by consequences of alcohol and drug use, and there is a huge emotional range of shame. You might feel shame over the loss of control of alcohol or drugs and think that it is some sort of moral issue. Understanding the disease of addiction helps you get a grip on this one. There may be shame concerning sex when you were doing meth or the DUI you got, or how there was something hurtful in your relationship. The list may seem as endless as the number of alcoholics and addicts who are in existence, but one thing is for sure—if you associate with people in recovery, you are likely to hear someone tell their story that sounds just like your story. This can be comforting, normalizing, and move you out of feeling isolated in your own mind about the conflicts that have come with the consequences of your alcohol and drug use. This is easy to say, but work on taking it easy, and talk about what is on your mind.

One issue with guilt and shame is that people around you could be hurt or angry about your use of alcohol or drugs and they either remind you or are reminders of what you do not feel good about. Sometimes this is very complex, and you may not get off very easily. Likewise, the solution may appear complex as well. On the surface, all of this is very reinforcing of guilt and shame. One thing is certain: It will get worse if you use again. One thing is also certain: Things will get better if you are clean and sober and working a good recovery program. This is the "keep it simple" aspect of the program. Despite all the complexities of what causes you guilt and shame, your life and the problems around it, you are ultimately guaranteed to get better if you are in recovery.

4. **Depression.** Three types of depression go along with substance abuse: (1) from the effects of substance abuse, (2) a reaction to consequences of substance abuse and adjustment reactions caused by crisis, and (3) clinical depression. Please realize that most people in early recovery feel some level of depression, and it just seems to go with the territory of getting clean and sober. It is a warning sign from the standpoint that if depression is not taken care of in some way, relapse may happen as a reaction to being depressed.

---

*Depression in Recovery*

- Caused by the effects of substance abuse

- Reaction to the consequences of substance abuse and adjustment reactions caused by crisis

- Clinical depression

---

The alcohol or drug you abused determines the severity of depression. There are other factors, such as intensity, frequency, duration of use, as well as personal characteristics that lead to greater or lesser proneness toward depression. Most alcoholics feel depression in the first days and weeks of sobriety but have major improvement by the end of the first month of sobriety. Some stimulant users, particularly methamphetamine, complain of some level of depression lasting longer. There is a lot of individual difference. The solution is the healing that comes with time being abstinent and the positive work you do that supports your sobriety.

The price of admission to recovery comes at a cost. What motivates people for recovery are the consequences caused by substance abuse, and like guilt and shame, there can be a depressive reaction. The talking cure: Talk about your feelings, which is a tough concept for a lot of people. Go to meetings. The "experience, strength, and hope" aspect of meetings helps normalize what happened as a result of using, provides support for getting through a difficult time, and leads to optimism about the future if you stay clean and sober.

Second, your lifestyle or habits, to some degree or another, have been centered around using and you did one thing: stop using. This one thing causes a lot of changes and adjustments. You have to adapt to the adjustments, which taps your personal and emotional resources. There are a lot of reactions to all of the change: You can get depressed, get overwhelmed with all of the change, "This requires too much. I am going to blow this off and go use again." Or you can take it one day at a time and do what you can do today to adjust to recovery and not worry too much about tomorrow.

Clinical depression requires professional evaluation. Clinical depression may have preceded your substance abuse or developed in the course of abusing alcohol or drugs. Sometimes people with clinical depression have a family history of it. Talk to your recovery staff member, or in group if you are concerned about being clinically depressed.

5. **Hopelessness vs. Acceptance.** Hopelessness can have two sides that can tie you up in a knot: one is the hopelessness about your ability to control alcohol or drugs; the other side is being hopeless in your ability to stay clean and sober. The hopelessness that comes with realization that you can't control alcohol or drugs is the result that your attempts to bargain with your addiction failed (cutting down, changing substances, reducing the number of days of use, cutting down the amount of time that you use, etc.). Feeling hopeless about your ability to control can be a good thing if it leads to the acceptance of the reality that you are an alcoholic or a drug addict.

Acceptance is the essential element that will lead you to the willingness of what you need to do to be sober. There is the acceptance of your disease of addiction. There is also the critical aspect of recovery, which is the acceptance of life on life's terms. One of the most famous quotes in the Big Book is on acceptance. It appears on page 449 of the third edition, the story of Dr. Paul O., doctor, alcoholic, and addict, and in the fourth edition it appears on page 417, "Acceptance Was the Answer."

*And acceptance is the answer to all my problems today. When I am disturbed, it is because I find some person, place, thing, or situation—some fact of my life—unacceptable to me, and I can find no serenity until I accept that person, place, thing, or situation as being exactly the way it is supposed to be at this moment. Nothing, absolutely nothing, happens in God's world by mistake. Until I could accept my alcoholism, I could not stay sober; unless I accept life completely on life's terms, I cannot be happy. I need to concentrate not so much on what needs to be changed in the world as on what needs to be changed in me and in my attitudes.*

Hopefulness is the profound belief and faith that you, in fact, have the ability to get clean and sober, the belief that your life will get better over time. Every suffering alcoholic and drug addict deserves to get clean and sober and to have a better life. You have suffered enough, despite how high or low your bottom was before making a decision to get into recovery or how many relapses you have experienced in the past. In large part, your ability to get clean and sober has to do with your belief that you can do it, plus the support and help you get as you navigate through the process. One problem is that many people feel that they will not be effective enough to make recovery happen. Strengthen your belief, your support for recovery, and feed that part of you that is hopeful with good thoughts.

6. **Self-pity vs. Recognition.** The reactions "Why is this happening to me?" and "This is not fair!" are major sources of self-pity. For certain, addictive illness is not fair. Nobody would wish to have it. You may feel that nobody really understands what you are going through. The fact is that everyone seems to go through some self-pity in early recovery, but be aware of it and don't get caught up in it.

"No one understands how tough it is for me to get sober and no one recognizes all the work I'm doing." You will ever get enough recognition from others for all of the hard work that is required to be clean and sober. Give yourself some recognition. When you get recognition from others, get it from people that truly understand addiction—others in recovery, your sponsor, and people who truly support your recovery.

The worst thing is "emotional kamikaze," which is to try to get recognition from people who are not going to give it to you or from people who are not ready to give it to you. You will end up feeling hurt and empty. An example is a family member who has never given you recognition, and he/she is still not going to give you recognition even though you are clean and sober and in recovery. Another example is an angry spouse who still harbors resentments and mistrust of you, and these feelings stand in the way of supporting the pain that you are going through and the work that you are doing to be sober.

Get recognition from people who truly understand addiction.

7. **Frustration and Anger.** Frustration and anger are experienced in so many different ways for the recovering person. Consequently, the following isn't meant to be the last word on how people experience frustration and anger in recovery, but rather an introduction to some ideas about it so you can start to think about how you can handle anger for a better recovery.

Anger in early recovery is common because of the oversensitivity caused by the effects of not using alcohol and drugs. Your nerve endings may feel a little raw. This is likely to result in overreactions to situations or difficulties tolerating frustration. Give yourself time to make the big adjustment to recovery and realize that it will get better.

Frustration generally happens because getting what you want is blocked in some way. A variation is that things may not be happening fast enough for you. These two variations happen countless times every day and are part of life. Dealing with frustration requires tolerance, patience, and acceptance of things as they are and not the way you want them to be. Too much frustration can result in anger.

Most people who are chronically angry are out of touch with their feelings. Feelings are either overcontrolled, tuned out, or if a feeling comes up, it may be singularly registered as anger. What about all of the other feeling possibilities besides feeling nothing or being angry? In recovery, learn about and articulate all the various feelings you actually have besides nothing or anger.

Anger can be a mask for fear or feeling hurt. A lot of the time fear or hurt are really the primary feelings, but the outward manifestation is anger. The next time that you are angry, stop and ask yourself, "What is the fear or what are the hurt feelings that are behind this anger?" For example, "I am fearful that I will not get what I want," "I am fearful that I will be out of control of the situation," "I am fearful that I will not be understood," "I feel humiliated and hurt, and I fear everyone will think I'm some type of fool," "I felt hurt by what you did," "I am hurt because you abused me," and so on.

Anger can be used to control others, in particular, when you feel out of control yourself. This is very common in people who rage or are control freaks. Anger is used as intimidation, and it is a form of being controlling and manipulative.

Building a case: Collect perceptions and cash them in for the prize that you are angling for. This one way of building up to using drugs or alcohol again. "I don't like what this person said." "I don't like what happened in that meeting." "These people don't know what they're talking about." "All of this is pissing me off. I'm outta here." This is alcoholic or drug addict thinking to build up enough anger to justify using again.

The energy from chronic anger can go in three basic directions. One, it can be internalized, or "stuffing feelings," which over time could lead to depression. Two, the intense form of externalized anger is rage. Three, self-destructive behavior could be rage turned inward. Anger experienced as depression, rage, or self-destruction are definitely relapse warning signs.

Deal with anger in healthy ways. Mostly focus on your part, as opposed to the major focus being on the other person or situation. (1) Objectively, what is the situation that is bothering you? (2) What are all the feelings that you have about it? (3) What do you contribute to the situation that is causing your anger, and what is reasonable to ask of others? (4) Engage in the solution by talking about it or find some other resolutions. Anger is a tough and sometimes complex emotion. Talk about your issues in the treatment groups, with your sponsor, and whatever venue you feel trust and support.

You will find it helpful in recovery to work on tolerance and the ability to tolerate frustration. Tolerance is not the same as "stuffing feelings" because tolerance is an active process of coping with frustration, whereas stuffing feelings is passive. Give yourself time: "This too shall pass." Look at what you can do to accept and tolerate the things that bother you and what you can do to make some changes so you are more comfortable. Use the Serenity Prayer to guide you and as a mantra to get you through frustrating times.

God grant me the serenity to accept the things I cannot change, the courage to change the things I can, and the wisdom to know the difference.

8. **Anxiety.** The physical effects of substance abuse can cause anxiety and agitation in early recovery. This type of anxiety usually subsides within a month of complete abstinence. Again, be patient with yourself.

Then there is the psychological aspect of being anxious. Mostly, this has to do with catastrophic thinking, thinking about the future, and thinking that all hell is going to break loose. Walking through your day might feel like you are walking through a minefield. Your next step might blow you up—attaching fear to future events. Are you a master at scaring yourself? This kind of anxiety is a time distortion, that is, thinking about events in the future that you have no control over and feeling scared about it. The answer: Focus on the present, be here and now, and not somewhere else. A history of not knowing what to expect usually causes this type of anxiety. For example, if you had a parent who was alcoholic and you did know whether he or she was going to be drunk or sober when you got home, and you became used to unpredictability. This causes anticipation and anxiety. It becomes chronic if it happened a lot, even though you are no longer exposed to the situation.

Anxiety might be called "excitement without oxygen." Notice your breathing when you are anxious. It will be shallow. People who experience panic breathe rapidly and shallowly but still feel that they are not getting air. Slow down when you are anxious and notice your breathing. Relax your stomach and abdomen, and breathe very slowly, deeply, and rhythmically into your stomach and abdomen. Focus on the present, and let go of thinking of the future. Tune in to where you are holding tension in your body and imagine that you can breathe out tension when you exhale.

There may be a lot of wreckage from your use of alcohol and drugs: financial, relationship, legal, work, health. This is a source of a lot of anxiety for people. Think about what you can do today about it. Get up tomorrow and again think of what you can do for that day, and let this process accumulate over time to get you some resolution. Work on making plans to solve your problems, without attaching unrealistic fears or expectations to the outcome. Do what you can do: "Make the plan; don't plan the outcome."

Some people get anxious because they basically feel incompetent and fear that their incompetency is about to get discovered. Feeling humiliated in some way in the past usually is the cause of this type of anxiety. Drinking and using drugs is often a cover for this one, and consequently some people feel exposed in sobriety. People with this type of anxiety problem do not have a realistic appraisal of themselves. Realistically figuring out your pluses and minuses might be one solution. The best solution is self-acceptance; come to believe that everyone is okay in their own way.

9. **Bored.** One alcoholic in recovery half-jokingly said, "Boredom is being devoid of drama." Are you a major risk taker and an excitement junkie? Boredom will be a liability for you in recovery unless you can transform your need for risk taking and drama. Have a blast in recovery, just make it healthy and avoid being self-destructive.

The "vacuum factor" is another cause of boredom in recovery. Using alcohol and drugs takes up a lot of time, and what happens when you stop? You have time on your hands. Time that what was once used for alcohol or drugs creates a time vacuum when you stop. What is one to do? Be involved in recovery activities: go to meetings, visit with people in recovery, see your sponsor, call people in recovery, read recovery literature, work on the steps, or go to recovery groups. The last thing you want to do is be with people you used alcohol or drugs with or be in places where you used to use, because these are major relapse triggers.

Addiction causes a narrowing of focus in life. The focus becomes more toward alcohol and drugs, to some exclusion of other things. Your number one priority should be recovery activities to help you with the vacuum factor, but also to expand your focus to the things that you missed out on because you were using. This is different for everybody, but examples are working on fitness, going to the gym, walking, running, cycling, eating some really good food, sports, being with your kids, home projects, fixing something, your hobby, doing other activities that does not involve substance use. Expand your focus to fun things in life, because one thing is for sure: If you can't learn to have fun in sobriety, you aren't going to stay sober.

---

If you can't learn how to have fun in sobriety, you aren't going to get sober.

---

10. **Resentments.** The word *resentment* has a Latin root meaning to re-feel . . . feel once and feel it over again. Someone has wronged, obstructed, or wounded you, and with resenting it, you feel the injuries again. AA's Big Book calls resentment the "number one offender." It also says, "It destroys more alcoholics than anything else." Each person has to find a way to deal with resentments. People say, "Let it go," but this takes some work and, like most things, is easier said than done.

Work on making progress at letting go of a particular resentment. Letting go of a resentment in no way means that you have to like that you were wronged. So many resentments have some elements of being irrational; that is because there are emotional parts to resentments. Figuring out rightness or wrongness is not as important as you feeling better. In other words, justifying your position is not as important as being more resolved and not as in much pain. You ultimately hurt yourself by holding on to resentment, and it tends to attract other negativity that will spoil your mood.

Resentment is something that you hold inside. One of the best ways to let go of resentment is to externalize it. Again, there is the talking cure. Talk about what is bothering you with someone who cares and who is also neutral. You will be frustrated if you talk with someone who doesn't care enough. You will probably get more resentful if you talk with someone who sides with you and inflames your resentment.

If appropriate, cope with the resentment directly by dealing with the person whom you feel wronged you. Try a three-part process: "This is what happened," "It made me feel . . .," "What I would like is . . ." You might want to practice this with someone before trying it on the person that you resent so you can iron out the bugs, or you may decide that the direct approach will not work and you will have to find another avenue to deal with the resentment.

AA's Big Book also suggests praying for someone whom you resent. You might say to yourself, "This sounds crazy. Why would I pray for somebody I resent . . . somebody who has hurt me?" It is one way to spiritually handle the resentment by having something outside yourself, your conception of a higher power, help you. It also helps you externalize the resentment and relieve yourself of holding it on the inside. Is this a one-time shot? It may not be a one-time effort, and it may take praying over a period of time to help you with your resentment. Not spiritually inclined? Do a healthy version of letting go what works for you. You might externalize the resentment by saying,

"What goes around, comes around." "Good deeds bring fortune; bad deeds bring misfortune."

An example of this is found in the famous excerpt from the Big Book which is contained in the story, "Freedom from Bondage." The writer said that her reprieve from abusing alcohol was running out. If she did not find a way to rid herself of resentment, she was going to get drunk, but she didn't want to drink ever again. The writer found a way that worked: "If you have a resentment you want to be free of, if you will pray for the person or thing that you resent, you will be free. If you will ask in prayer for everything you want for yourself to be given to them, you will be free. Ask for their health, their prosperity, their happiness, and you will be free. Even when you don't really want it for them and your prayers are only words and you don't mean it, go ahead and do it anyway. Do it every day for two weeks, and you will find you have come to mean it and want it for them, and you will realize that where you used to feel bitterness and resentment and hatred, you now feel compassionate understanding and love."

11. **Loneliness:** Are you basically an isolator? Getting loaded is surely a distraction from feeling lonely. Get sober, then what? Were you using alcohol or drugs with people and your main source of connection? You will probably eventually use again if you spend time with people who use. You may also be in that gap between disconnecting with your old using friends and lifestyle and developing new friends in recovery, along with a recovery support system. This might leave you feeling lonely at times.

Some people in early sobriety question their social skills or feel a little anxiety about connecting with new people. You may feel alone, but you are not alone. You are not the only one . . . everyone seems to go through this at some degree or another. Go early to meetings and stay late. Talk to one person to get started. People in early recovery sometimes complain about cliques at twelve-step meetings. Sometimes these exist, and at other times people go out of their way to greet the newcomer to the program.

Get a sponsor or temporary sponsor who has availability and time to talk with you. At first, you may want or need to connect every day with your sponsor. Figure out a slice of time each day when you can connect. Cellular technology helps with connecting with your sponsor. Go to meetings with your sponsor. The recovery groups are a fairly easy way to connect with others because of the structure of the program.

The best way to deal with loneliness is by planning your time. A setup for loneliness is not planning your time. You might not think of it in advance, forget to do it, or think that it is not that important. Then you find yourself with time, being alone and lonely. Then there is the vulnerability and the urge to contact your old friend: the drug or the booze. Going to meetings is always a good fallback position.

12. **Unresolved stress.** Unresolved stress might come up in recovery because it is no longer being covered up by the use of alcohol or drugs. This could be a posttraumatic stress disorder (PTSD) or some other form of harm to you from the past. The major offenders are emotional, physical, or sexual abuse. Dealing with these issues in early recovery is a tricky navigation between a rock and a hard place. Most people do not have enough recovery to go through the feelings about the abuse, yet without alcohol or drugs, the feelings sometimes spontaneously come up. Please discuss it with your CDS case manager or one of the therapists in the program to develop a plan, given your particular situation.

13. **Feeling stuck.** What causes you to feel stuck, and do you have anywhere to turn? It would be amazing if you never felt stuck in recovery, but here are various times that feeling stuck naturally occurs in the evolution of getting clean and sober. Ask yourself what it means for you. If you are really involved in a program of recovery, it may mean that you have to regroup.

For example, your sponsor has been very forthright in working with you to march through the steps, and all of a sudden you hit a snag. What is that about? It may mean that you have worked though some of the steps, but they need to be more thoroughly integrated before you can move on. A simple solution is to review the steps that you have worked on and see how you might embrace them more fully before you take the next step.

Feeling stuck has to do with readiness. You need to make a change, but it is not happening. Recovery is dynamic, and there seems to always be some element of movement. Are you ready to move onto the next stage of your recovery? One example is the fourth step, where many people feel stuck when they approach it. There may be two things going on. One is whether you feel that you have actually digested the first three steps of the program, and the other is whether you feel emotionally ready for the fourth step. Regroup and move on. What does being stuck represent for you?

There may be other areas of your life where you feel stuck, where there is some sort of obstacle that is stalling your progress. The obstacle may be vague or apparent, but there is some sort of variation on feeling that you have nowhere to turn. Figure out what exactly is making you feel stuck. The other side of it is that everyone, to a greater or lesser degree, has options. What are they, from the irrational to the logical? Do something that is reasonable for you, something that makes sense. Talk it over with someone you trust.

C. **Behavioral Warning Signs.** Most of the time, what you think and feel is not as important as what you actually do. For example, you may feel a compulsion to use, but what do you really do about it? What are those things that you do on a consistent basis that lead you to recovery and sobriety? Behavioral recovery signs and behavioral relapse warning signs are objective measures of how you are doing in your recovery program. Behavioral relapse warning signs naturally occur in the course of recovery, and what you do about them determines whether you stay sober or relapse. Sometimes relapse behaviors occur unconsciously or automatically, so developing self-awareness is key to recovery and avoiding relapse.

1.  **Loss of constructive planning.** Planning is one of most central and important things in your recovery. Plan your time, plan your recovery. You may be unconsciously planning a relapse if you don't have a plan for what you are going to specifically do for your recovery. Use your daily planner to nail down your recovery plan for the day or week: What hours and days are you going to meetings, meeting your sponsor, doing recovery reading, connecting with people in recovery, and so on. Keep recovery your first priority, but constructive planning also means to fit in the other parts of your life: family, job, and the nuts and bolts of daily living.

    > Plan your time, plan your recovery.

    Scheduling and planning your time helps with not having time weigh too heavy on your hands. Scheduling your time is essential, especially in early recovery, and particularly at the times of the day when you were most likely to use alcohol or drugs.

    You may have a plan established for recovery, and then somewhere down the road it doesn't seem as necessary or as important to you. Maybe you feel like you have graduated from recovery, like graduating from school or finishing a class. Recovery is never a done deal, where you get a certificate and move on with a feeling of being cured.

Need drives what your plan should be and should dictate the level of intensity for your plan. Loss of an appropriate plan for you is a critical warning sign of relapse.

2.   **Relationships.** New romantic relationships too early in recovery can be a major threat to sobriety. It is easy for the "detox relationship" to replace the alcohol or the drug and become an addictive relationship, where the alcoholic or addict obsesses on the other person and may have compulsive behaviors that erode recovery. You have probably heard the guideline in AA: "No new relationships in the first year of sobriety." This guideline is for a lot of reasons. New relationships are usually such a nice high and shake you up in all kinds of wonderful ways . . . Can you handle it and stay sober? The intoxicating effects of a new relationship can trigger obsessive and compulsive behaviors to use alcohol or drugs. You are changing in positive ways in recovery, starting to feel good about yourself, learning new things, and maybe feeling some passion in life. Your juices may be flowing and you feel attracted to someone. There may be the impulse to jump. Start to talk about it with people in seasoned recovery if you start thinking about having a new relationship.

Relationships are emotionally charged. Learning to deal with feelings and emotions in early recovery is a major undertaking, and throwing a new relationship in the mix creates a ride that may be too wild to sustain sobriety. Maybe relationships have been difficult in the past and you meet someone who strokes your ego. Who wouldn't be vulnerable to that? There is the high of the new relationship, then there is the low when the complications start to seep in. It is always easier to get into a relationship than to get out of one . . . One way to cope is to start using again.

Most people in recovery are trying to iron out conflicts about dependency and control. Of course this relates to drugs and alcohol, but it also relates to relationships:

- Needing someone to validate you because you are having trouble validating yourself

- Wanting to be taken care of

- Having the need to take care of someone else when you are just learning to take care of yourself

- Holding another person captive

- Controlling to get what you want

- Wanting things on your terms and in your time frame

- Jealousies or some other form of insecurity start creeping in

The list is endless when it comes to relationship conflicts about dependency and control. The best idea is to get some mileage in recovery and feel some emotional maturity to feel whole enough to start a new relationship. Also, almost everyone has some problem or issue with sex. Are you ready to face that one yet?

**A spouse that still drinks or uses drugs.** You are already in a relationship and your partner drinks or uses—either like a sane person or like an addict. What is one to do? The first step is not to deny that it is a major issue. Exposure to alcohol or drugs is a major offender of sobriety, as well as being with or relating with someone who is using. Wouldn't you like to be normal and use with them? How about kissing someone with alcohol on their breath or having sex with someone who is wired or stoned? This situation is fraught with so many complications, and there is never a totally simple solution, except for one—be honest with yourself, talk with others, and develop a plan,

**Enduring conflicts and codependent roles.** There is a piece in the Big Book of AA that discusses the alcoholic's use of alcohol as being like a tornado in the life of the family. The person stops drinking and makes the understatement, "Gee, the wind has died down." We get clean, we get sober, and we start to feel good about ourselves; we get new friends in recovery, and we have more energy. In most cases, our spouses and family members don't get established in recovery so fast. They are hurt, angry and have big problems with trust. "I am feeling better. Why can't they just get over it and move on?" There certainly isn't any quick fix for this one.

The spouse or family members generally need to begin to have an understanding of addictive illness and also develop an understanding of their part of the "family disease of addiction." The family disease simply means that addiction affects not just the alcoholic or drug addict, but many others. This results in unhealthy roles in the family being developed in order to compensate in various ways for how the addiction gets played out in the family. These roles can have an enduring quality and may not quickly change when the alcoholic or addict gets into recovery. The spouse and family have to examine their roles and agendas. It is easy for the alcoholic or drug addict to regress into old addictive patterns if the codependent doesn't change. Codependency groups and Al-Anon are important for the family's recovery and, by extension, helpful for the alcoholic and drug addict's recovery. New roles and problems with trust take time and effort to change.

3. **Drama: Positive versus negative.** Drama can either be toward recovery or away from it—the drama of recovery versus the drama that creates the instability for recovery. The drama of recovery is the engagement, animation, passion, and connection that you invest in the recovery process. It is navigating conflict and experiencing personal transformation as result, which adds character and depth to your life. The drama of recovery is the new story and new history you create in your life.

Negative drama, or "high drama" is a relapse warning sign because it cuts away at recovery. It is the creation of problems, conflicts, and negative situations . . . the addict mind unconsciously at work in mysterious ways. Examples are arguments and fault finding in others or the manipulation of a situation to manufacture some sort of tempest in a teapot. Blame the situation or person with the usual agenda is to find some justification to go use again.

There are some people in recovery who experience high drama as somewhat of an enduring personality issue, much like what is described in step six of the Twelve Steps, where a person has tendencies toward drama. Step six calls it a "defect of character." What is one to do if it is an enduring personality trait and also a relapse warning sign? Recovery is truly a program of progress, not perfection. This is what is meant in step six when it says that one becomes entirely ready to have defects of character removed. It doesn't mean that enduring personality problems are instantly removed; it means that there is a readiness to make progress in the direction of being a healthier human being, to have greater insight into your personal behaviors, and to work on having better judgment for the decisions that you make.

4. **Compulsive behaviors.** Having negative compulsive behaviors when abstinent from chemicals is a variation of switching addictions. Compulsive behaviors are self-defeating, distracting from recovery, and can actually activate the addictive part of your brain associated with the reward system, which is associated with addiction. Compulsive behaviors are warning signs of relapse, but they can also trigger a relapse. The major offenders are gambling, compulsive sex, increased use of caffeine, spending money for the thrill of it, compulsive eating, Internet addiction, and so on.

There are positive compulsive behaviors in recovery, like going to meetings and engaging in other recovery behaviors. Some critics say with a negative tone, "Going to all of those meetings is like switching the meeting for the drug." The critic has it wrong and right. The wrong part is being judgmental, being critical, having a negative tone, and not having the realization that going to a lot of meetings allows the recovering person not to only fill the void left by not using substances, but also to learn from others how to live sober. So if you are a compulsive person by the nature of your addiction, then going to a lot of meetings is a very adaptive and functional thing to do in recovery, and why not? Exercise and other positive health practices are fantastic ways to bridle those compulsive energies.

5. **Dishonesty.** Dishonesty is a critical warning sign. One of the most famous parts of the recovery literature reflects this and says, "Rarely have we seen a person fail who has thoroughly followed our path. Those who do not recover are people who cannot or will not completely give themselves to this simple program, usually men and women who are constitutionally incapable of being honest with themselves." What is discussed is the necessity for "rigorous honesty." Constantly do an honesty check with yourself. The first step of rigorous honesty is working on being honest with yourself. Then, by extension, you work on being honest with others. Start to examine how you might be manipulative, and begin to be more accurate about how you perceive reality and how you present reality to others.

Self-honesty is such a cornerstone of recovery that the saying "To thine own self be true" appears on every AA anniversary medallion, or "chip." The saying originated in Shakespeare's *The Tragedy Hamlet, Prince of Denmark* (1602). In this drama, Hamlet has to face problems of duty, personal morality, and ethics, which are mirrored in how he deals with his despair, feelings of frustration, hopes, and fears. (Sounds parallel to recovery, doesn't it?)

> "This above all: to thine own self be true,
>
> And it must follow, as the night the day,
>
> Thou canst not then be false to any man."

A part of the disease of addiction is that reality gets distorted on all kinds of twisted ways. And why? So you can use. I lie to myself and others so I can continue to do my thing with my alcohol or my drug.

I lie to myself to make it okay for me, and I manipulate others so I can hold on to my stuff. Lying to myself and others can get as habitual as the use of the alcohol or drug. The problem is that I have the tendency to habitually lie to myself even though I am abstinent because it is ingrained. I'll tell myself all kinds of good tales to lead me back to using again. The problem of partial truths is the reason that one needs rigorous honesty to be completely truthful with oneself and to recover. The reason is that partial truths are still lies: Omissions are another major way to be dishonest.

Truthfulness with oneself is really the key. However, sometimes complete truthfulness and openness with others can be a real problem. This is addressed step nine of the Twelve Steps where it discusses making amends: "Make direct amends to such people wherever possible, except when to do so would injure them or others." The step goes on to say that "complete disclosures do them or others more harm than good." The step points out that one shouldn't be completely open with others where it will do harm. At the same time, you can be completely honest with yourself because you will have identified the persons you have harmed and will have worked out an appropriate way to make an amends. This is not a lie by omission, but rather exercising judgment for the greater good. Most of the time, these distinctions can be very confusing, but the very good news is that this road has been navigated countless times by others that have gone before you in recovery. There are good maps out there for figuring this out. Count on others who know about recovery to be your sounding board and to give feedback.

6.  **Isolation versus solitude.** Isolation is about being detached in the negative sense, and solitude is about the need for privacy. Isolation is a central symptom of addiction and a hallmark warning sign of relapse. It may be a gradual or abrupt way of cutting yourself off from your recovery and others in recovery. You may have heard the saying, "Addiction is a disease of isolation." Being alone within yourself and feeling that personal inner drive of how you can give to yourself by using. A scenario: "I have to get people off my back so I can use. I need to have some space, and I need to have some hideouts." In many senses, the disease of addiction is intricately connected with isolation. You may have also felt isolated when you were using with others because the connection was about the drug or the alcohol, and you were in your own orbit without feeling really connected . . . other than feeling connected because you got loaded together.

Starting to isolate is generally linked to regressing to old behaviors. You don't have control over the disease of addiction, but you have control over the decision of raising the threshold of recovery to prevent relapse. One solid way of staying clean and sober is to stay connected. Isolation is a symptom of losing the decision to stay sober and cutting yourself off from others who can help you stay sober. It creates an opportunity to use, which may be a conscious or unconscious plan in the making. Isolation is like having the addiction whisper in your ear that you don't need help and seduce you back to getting high . . . and the misery or consequences that you experienced before.

Isolation can also be one symptom of depression. Think about whether you might be having the blues that everyone experiences from time to time: depression which results from detox from alcohol or drugs, some transient depression, or that you actually might be depressed. Isolation that is associated with depression can be quite immobilizing. Get help with therapists in your recovery group to sort this out and get a plan to help you. Keep mobilized and connected, even if you don't feel like it. Doing what you don't feel like doing is the best remedy in this case.

**Solitude is different.** Think of prayer, meditation, study, contemplation, or being with yourself in all kinds of wonderful ways that are particularly nourishing for you. It is the need for personal privacy for whatever purpose. The need for solitude is not driven by addiction, but the need to have time to take things in or to rejuvenate yourself.

7. **Alienating people who can help you.** Alienating others is an addictive and sometimes crafty way to push people that represent recovery away. It may be preceded by drumming up some sort of resentment or judgment to justify alienating someone that could help you stay sober. "I can do it my way. They don't really have a clue about it." Alienating people who can help you is usually directed at others in recovery, professionals who work with chemically dependent people, and so on. You might have problems with someone and that might equate to an all-or-nothing "I'm outta here." It is one way to develop an excuse to use. Don't avoid problems if you have a genuine issue. For example, if your sponsor doesn't make him or herself available enough for you, talk with your sponsor about it. You can work something out with the sponsor, or if you need to, get another one who is available.

8. **Procrastination.** "Why do today what I can put off until tomorrow?" Some alcoholics and drug addicts got a lot of practice at procrastination when using because they have kept putting things off because of using.

One type of procrastination is "I'll quit using tomorrow." It is amazing how tomorrow can add up a lot of days, weeks, or years.

In terms of recovery, procrastination is one form of sabotaging yourself because it undermines recovery. In some ways, procrastination can be about avoidance and passivity about taking care of business. Procrastination takes countless forms. For example, putting off going to meetings because you worked all day and you are tired and you just want to stay home. Of course you were never too tired to drink or use drugs. Putting off calling people in recovery or facing the resolution of resentments that come up on the fourth step are other typical examples of procrastination in recovery. Identify what you are procrastinating about, then ask yourself, "What am I avoiding and why?"

9. **Secrets.** Do you have something that is bugging you, but you feel that you cannot talk about it because of shame, humiliation, or because some sort of fallout that will cause major consequences for you or somebody else? Privacy is a very important thing in life, but then there are secrets that you keep inside that make you sick . . . the secrets that would be ultimately harmful to your ability to stay sober. How about, "You are as sick as your secrets." There are things that you probably would not want on the front page of the newspaper, so you need a confidant who can handle discussing your secret(s), who will respect your need for confidentiality, and whom you can trust.

10. **Rejecting input.** "Contempt prior to investigation" is having a predetermined judgment about what is not going to work for you. It is also being naive, not willing to be informed, or being in denial of what you need to do in the process of recovery. "I'm know that I'm an addict, but I don't need to do this or that to be in recovery!" This usually has to do with resistance, defensiveness, and problems with willingness. You hurt, but you don't want to change to alleviate the problems that hurt you. "What do they know, anyway?" Being in recovery is about willingness and being open to being helped by people who have been down the path and know the lay of the land of recovery.

11. **Complacency.** Complacency is about the mismatch between what you need to do to maintain sobriety versus feeling smug or having a false sense of security about abstinence and being unaware of the danger of relapse lurking in the background. Complacency is a major offender for people who have achieved some sustainable sobriety, but who then begin to minimize what is needed to maintain recovery: "I stopped going to my meetings and drifted away from my program."

"My sponsor moved away, and I didn't get another one because I already worked the steps." "I had time pressures with my job and didn't feel that I need to spend as much time with the program. I forgot my priorities." "I really forgot that I am only one drink away from a drunk." These are some of the statements from people who have relapsed because of complacency.

Recovery is never a sure thing, and you have to keep some degree of vigilance to hang on to it. As the saying goes: "Addiction is cunning, baffling, and powerful . . . and it is patient." What you need to do to stay sober may become less clear after all the intensity of early recovery dies down. The level of involvement (in terms of meeting attendance and recovery activities) depends on the person. The later steps of the program provide guidance and help avoid complacency—continue to take a personal inventory and improve a sense of conscious contact; helping others in recovery will help you maintain your recovery.

12. **Associate with people who use.** Now this is a major-league warning sign: You feel like being with your old using buddies. What would make you feel like that, and what is the natural thing to do with your old friends? Wanting to use when you are with your old friends is automatic, and not using while with them is a tough proposition. You could probably not use, but if you continually put yourself in harm's way, it may be like the old AA saying, "If you keep going to the barbershop, you will eventually get a haircut."

The transition to a sober lifestyle is difficult, particularly with all of the social shifts that it requires. Start to connect with new sober friends, have phone lists, and call them. Strengthen your existing relationships that truly support your recovery.

## WARNING SIGNS                    ## ACTIONS AND SOLUTIONS

1. _____    A. _____
                                B. _____
                                C. _____

2. _____    A. _____
                                B. _____
                                C. _____

3. _____    A. _____
                                B. _____
                                C. _____

4. _____    A. _____
                                B. _____
                                C. _____

5. _____    A. _____
                                B. _____
                                C. _____

6. _____    A. _____
                                B. _____
                                C. _____

7. _____    A. _____
                                B. _____
                                C. _____

8. _____    A. _____
                                B. _____
                                C. _____

9. _____    A. _____
                                B. _____
                                C. _____

10. _____    A. _____
                                B. _____
                                C. _____

# References:

Alcoholics Anonymous (1976). *Alcoholics anonymous (Third Ed.).* New York: AA World Services.

Alcoholics Anonymous (2001). *Alcoholics anonymous (Fourth Ed.).* New York: AA World Services.

Alcoholics Anonymous (1953). *Twelve steps and twelve traditions.* New York: AA World Services.

McCausland, W. S. (1984). Unpublished doctoral dissertation, *Alcoholism treatment participation as a function of MMPI cluster type and life stress.* Ann Arbor: University Microfilms International.

# SUCCESSFUL RECOVERY

## Support Systems for Recovery

---

**Orientation. Social Support Networks.**

- How does your social network support your recovery?

- Know the positive and negative support systems for recovery.

- Identify and evaluate your support systems for recovery.

---

**A.  How does your social network support your recovery?**

   **1.  Social Support Systems Are Defining.**

- The quality and type of your support system says a lot about you.

- Your support system defines you—your identity. In a black-and-white sense, this goes in one of two ways. You will have a support system that reflects recovery if you truly identify as being a person in recovery. You will have a support system that encourages using alcohol or drugs if in your gut you are still an active user. What about shades of gray? It doesn't go both ways. You will end up using alcohol or drugs if you have one support system that supports recovery and another one that supports using.

- Your support system contributes to defining what you will feel. We have to face the fact that as human beings, our feelings are strongly influenced by other people. Positive people bring us up. Inspirational people compel us to be influenced by them. People practicing strong and attractive recovery programs make us feel like wanting recovery. Old friends who used to support our alcohol or drug use probably will make us feel like using.

- Your support system defines what you will do. Relative to recovery, support systems sanction either using or not using. They are quite influential. You are likely to be sober if you hang out in AA. You are likely to use if you hang out with your old using buddies.

- Does it support your getting clean and sober?

- Or does it support your getting loaded?

## 2. Supports and Friends.

- Do you have a full and healthy set of relationships? Do your relationships have the strength and satisfy your needs for recovery?

- Relying on too few people or on people who are not strong themselves will result in not satisfying your needs in recovery. You will be more vulnerable to relapse.

## B. Positive and Negative Support Systems for Recovery.

1. **Positive: Supports recovery.** Examples are twelve-step groups, CDS groups, your sponsor, family and friends with a clear vision about recovery whose support isn't tainted by negative feelings toward you, and so on. Sometimes people who do not even know that you are in recovery will provide very positive support. These are the people who are naturally positive, nurturing, and bring you up by just being around them.

> People in a positive support system help you sustain recovery.

2. **Negative: Supports using.** Examples are old using buddies, a spouse who still uses, kids who have a lot of negative feelings toward you, kids who use themselves, family members who stress you out, or a job situation that doesn't support recovery.

> People in a negative support system undermine your recovery and make you vulnerable to relapse.

3. **Seems negative but is positive.** Examples are being forced into treatment by someone who represents authority. You might resent authority or have conflicts about authority. Consequently, you might feel resistant or put up a wall. Being forced may feel negative, but the positive part is that it gets you in the door. Examples are being forced by the courts, probation officers, your employer, or your doctor. Having someone else provide the initial motivation for your recovery is okay, as long as you make the shift and ultimately realize that recovery is a positive move for you.

Someone else might motivate you to get sober, but ultimately you have to do it for yourself.

4. **Seems positive, but is negative.** Examples are a spouse and family members who are angry toward you, are controlling, and need to be in their own recovery program, like Al-Anon. In theory, your spouse and family should be naturally supportive, but in practice, this doesn't always happen. This could be the result of a lot of history of your alcohol or drug use, massive feelings of mistrust toward you, and reactive overcontrolling behaviors toward you. It could also be the result of your spouse growing up in an alcoholic family, then marrying you. Your spouse may actually have a hard time handling you getting sober because living in an alcoholic family is so ingrained, and changing to a recovery lifestyle is significant. The result for you is to not have any illusions about these folks and their true abilities to be really supportive. The takeaway message is that they probably have their own recovery programs that they need to engage in.

Another example is the old using buddy or drug dealer who says one thing but represents something else. "I'm glad that you are getting help because you were such a mess," he or she might say, but the person still uses, and connecting with him or her is a trigger to use yourself.

May appear supportive, but in reality sabotage your recovery

C. **Identify and Evaluate Your Support System for Recovery.**

1. **Friendship Checklist.**

   • What are you receiving from people in your life?

   • The following checklist may help you look more closely at current sources of support.

   • It is okay if you are not able to say yes to all the items.

   • The list may be vital for what you need to work on.

| Do you have: | Yes | No | Who? |
|---|---|---|---|
| People you trust, who won't manipulate you for their own | | | |
| purposes? | | | |
| People with whom you can have healthy fun and recreation? | | | |
| People who share your own special recreation interests and | | | |
| hobbies? | | | |
| People to learn from: | | | |
| About work and career? | | | |
| About everyday life? | | | |
| About recovery from alcohol and drugs? | | | |
| People you can lean on who are also working on recovery? | | | |
| Someone with whom you have an intimate and loving | | | |
| relationship? | | | |
| People with whom you can discuss personal and serious concerns? | | | |
| People you can count on in a crisis? | | | |
| Sensible people who will confront you, in a caring way, with | | | |
| problems that they see in your behavior or mistakes in your | | | |
| thinking? | | | |
| People who participate with you in spiritual or religious activities? | | | |
| Good people whom you are comfortable with and are near enough | | | |
| that you can drop by easily when you really need some company? | | | |

2. **Exercise: What Is Your Support System?**

- Use the pie chart and write down all the members of your support system, whether or not they positively or negatively influence your recovery.

- Then, circle those that truly support your recovery.

- Next, list ways that you can strengthen your support system.

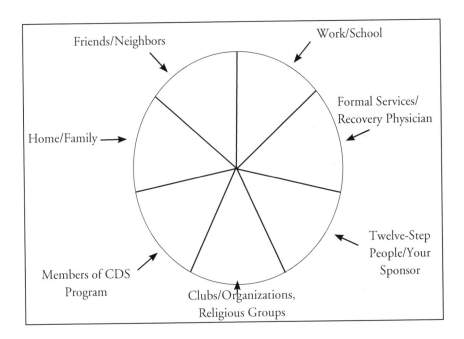

3. **How I could strengthen my support system:**

1. _____

_____

2. _____

_____

3. _____

_____

4. _____

_____

5. _____

_____

6. _____

_____

7. _____

_____

# Reference

University of California, San Diego, Center for Addiction Research, Training and Application (2001). Support and friendship checklist. *In* Relapse prevention: the sequence of steps.

# SUCCESSFUL RECOVERY

## The Disease Concept

**Orientation. The Disease Concept of Addiction.** The following section provides support for understanding how addiction is actually a disease. This understanding is critical for helping you during the ongoing process of recovery.

- A. Diagnosis: control, compulsion, and consequences.

- B. Chronic, progressive, and irreversible, and part of the disease is denying you have it.

- C. Brain disease has many influences:

  - ✓ Genes—inherited

  - ✓ The brain and making decisions: The "executive brain" becomes damaged

  - ✓ Brain chemistry that produces euphoria—the brain reward system

  - ✓ Brain becomes rewired for addiction.

- D. Psychological factors:

  - ✓ The existence vs. myth of an "addictive personality"

  - ✓ Risk avoiders, risk takers, and addiction

  - ✓ Stress, "soothability," and addiction

- E. "Cure" vs. management of addiction: What is the goal of recovery?

## Introduction. Labeling addiction as a disease is not a new concept.

- Benjamin Rush, MD labeled alcoholism as a disease in the 1700s.

- The disease model of addiction provides the framework for AA and other twelve-step groups. Sometimes it is referred to as a "mental obsession plus a physical allergy."

- The disease model is validated through current science. *No*

**A. How do you diagnose that you have it?**

1. Knowing and acknowledging that you have an addiction is critical because then you can take the next step and do something about it. It is typical to deny the addiction through fallacious logic: "Alcoholics and drug addicts look like this and do that. I don't do this or that. Therefore, I'm not an alcoholic or a drug addict."

2. The key element of addiction is the continued use of a substance despite negative consequences.

3. The three C's of addiction:

   • **Control:** This lack of control comes in many forms, but the basic one is not being able to control the amount you use. It may not be every time you use, and you may not be able to predict when you will be in control or not be in control. You think you should cut down. You may want or try to stop altogether, but you can't. You stop, but then go back to using.

   • **Compulsion:** Use is based on the obsessive need and irresistible impulse to use. At times, you may not even want to use, but you do it anyway. A form of obsession and compulsion is the focusing of your attention on the alcohol or the drug and narrowing your attention on your family, work, or other interests.

   • **Consequences:** A typical scenario for beginning a pattern of abuse or dependence is to have a consequence. Continuing to use despite negative consequences is what separates addicts from nonaddicts. Those consequences come down the pike in various ways, but generally they have to do with relationships, legal issues, work, health, or some other impact on your functioning.

**B. Additional factors in addiction**

   • **Primary illness:** Chemical dependency should be considered the primary disease when it is intertwined with another problem, such as an emotional or physical difficulty. The reason is the other difficulties cannot be effectively treated until the chemical dependency is dealt with because of the impact chemical dependency has on emotional and physical functioning.

The reasons for starting alcohol or drug use become a secondary issue once you have become addicted. For example, self-medicating with alcohol or drugs to cope with emotional distress or physical pain is a common avenue to addiction, but once addiction is established, it develops a complicated life of its own. At this point, addiction becomes the primary illness despite why substances were used in the first place. The power of addiction is so strong that it will continue to exist even if the initial problem disappears.

Some examples of psychological problems that coincide with addiction are depression, anxiety, stress, having suicidal thoughts, another form of emotional problem, the consequences of emotional or physical abuse, and so on. Substance abuse causes all types of medical problems, and those organ systems that are most vulnerable are the cardiovascular system, the gastrointestinal system, and the central and peripheral nervous systems. Accidents, assaults, and other physical damage as a consequence of substance use are also considered medical problems, and they may result in the need for medical treatment. To emphasize, all of these problems can't be effectively helped until addictive illness is treated first or in conjunction with one another.

- **Progressive:** It gets worse, not better. The worsening of the disease includes the physical, psychological, social, and spiritual realms. Addiction can also become worse during times of abstinence because of "shadow progression," the phenomenon which occurs when the disease of addiction progresses despite you're not using any alcohol or drugs. Shadow progression is when you find the addiction actually worsens when you go back to using after a period of sobriety.

- **Chronic:** There is no cure. Once the disease is established, it doesn't go away. Any mind-altering substance can't be used safely because it will either lead to addiction to that drug or lead you back to your drug of choice.

- **Fatal:** We are all going to die at some point, but it is going to happen faster if you don't stop using. Examples of what makes it fatal are physical problems, accidents, suicide, and other substance-related misadventures, such as being in the wrong place at the wrong time.

- **Denial:** Part of the disease is a denial of the effects that substance use has on your life.

## C. Brain disease has many influences.

### 1. Genetic scenario #1: Inherit the addiction.

1.  The disease of addiction has a genetic component and tends to run in families. There isn't one specific gene, but several genes that act in various ways that contribute to developing addiction. It can skip a generation.

2.  Twin studies: With identical twins, if one is alcoholic, 53 percent of the time, the other will share the addiction. For fraternal twins, it is 28 percent.

3.  Adoption studies: Nature (genes) versus nurture (environment). Adoptees with addicted biological parents were four times more likely to develop addiction than adoptees with nonaddicted biological parents. Both grew up in a nonaddict household.

4.  Gender of the parent versus gender of the child. A female can pass the disease onto her son, and a male can pass it onto his daughter. Gender doesn't matter.

5.  Genetic influence is not drug specific. For example, if you have an alcoholic parent, you could have another drug of choice, such as cocaine or marijuana. Some people who grow up in alcoholic families say, "I'm never going to be an alcoholic," but then use and get addicted to another substance.

6.  Inherited genes are a risk factor.

    - Genetic influence is a risk factor and not disease in itself.

    - On average, genetics account for about 50 percent of the addiction, the remainder is psychological, social, and environmental.

    - Diathesis-stress model of addiction: "Diathesis" = genes. "Stress" = everything else that mobilizes genetic potential to create addictive illness.

    - The stronger the disease is in one generation, the more likely it is to be transmitted to the next generation.

### 2. The Executive Brain.

1. In general, the "executive brain" is a term that describes the part of your brain that makes decisions about how to do things, and it also has to do with judgment.

2. Using alcohol or drugs can hurt this part of the brain, and affect the quality of making decisions. For example, it can hurt the following abilities:

   - Judgment

   - Memory

   - Concentration

   - Ability to control impulses

   - Ability to plan

   - Ability to organize

3. This is important to know for a number of reasons:

   - Decisions that you might think are good decisions might, in reality, be poor decisions: "My best thinking got me here."

   - It doesn't matter if you are the alcoholic or drug addict with the highest IQ on the face of the earth—it can still be a problem.

   - Get feedback from others in the know.

   - Take time to make decisions, avoid doing things on impulse that could have negative outcomes, and talk about various aspects of a decision before making it.

   - Be willing to get direction from others about recovery, as opposed to coming up with your own customized version of what you think might work. An example is dropping out of treatment or twelve-step programs and trying recovery through some alternative plan or through self-will. Another example is not getting rid of alcohol or drugs in your house or thinking it's okay to hang around with people who use.

   - The brain recovers with abstinence, but it takes some time.

## 3. Dopamine: The brain's euphoria chemical

1. Dopamine is a neurotransmitter, which means it is a chemical that is released from one nerve cell to communicate to another nerve cell. Dopamine is the transmitter that is responsible for

feelings of euphoria or elation. Under natural conditions, it gets released when you eat something, have sex, drink (even nonalcoholic) liquids, etc. Dopamine is also released under other normal conditions. For example, having a piece of chocolate, getting a little blast if someone tells you that you are looking good, having a good laugh, etc. Generally, if something feels rewarding, there is probably a little dopamine involved.

2. Survival is why dopamine and feeling rewarded came about in the first place. Eating and keeping hydrated feels like a reward because of the pleasurable effects that dopamine gives. You keep on doing it. The person survives. Likewise, sex feels rewarding because of the pleasurable effects that result from the release of dopamine. We have sex, then children, and the species survives.

3. Use drugs to survive? All drugs of abuse affect dopamine transmission, whether upper, downer, or narcotizer. Addiction proceeds when alcohol or drugs hijack the dopamine system in the brain. This may lead people to compulsive use, where you feel like you are using to survive rather than just to get high. For these reasons, dopamine is sometimes referred to as the "master molecule of addiction."

4. Magnitudes of dopamine: The degree of addictiveness of a drug is relative to its magnitude of effect.

- Food: spike of 100 to 150 units

- Sex at point of orgasm: 200 units

- Alcohol: 100–200 units

- Cocaine: 350 units

- Methamphetamine: 1,250 units

## 4. Voluntary drug use changes and becomes compulsive drug use.

1. **First it is a choice.** Take the alcohol or the drug, and it sends dopamine though a system in the brain called the reward pathway. You get high.

2. **It becomes compulsive use.** Compulsive use happens when there are alterations in the brain that cause it to get rewired to being addicted. It then becomes an addicted brain.

3. **Chemical factors that produce motivation to use which result in addiction.**

- Euphoria makes you want to keep on doing it.

- Not using it makes you want to use. This includes the bad effects of withdrawal and wanting to self-medicate to avoid the feeling of withdrawal.

5. **Genetic Scenario #2: Developing addiction through changes in the genes.**

   1. Substance use causes certain genes to get turned on and off.*

      - Tolerance occurs when using creates the need to use more.

      - Sensitivity occurs within a few days of not using.

      - This causes a vulnerability to using because of a sensitivity of cues, memories, using associations—long after abstention.

      - This sensitization caused by alterations in the genes is associated with craving and underlies compulsive drug and alcohol seeking.

*CREB transcription factor – a signaling protein which turns genes on and off.

   2. Other gene changes that are more stable and enduring.**

      - Gradual and progressive changes in the brain reward pathway occur over time with substance abuse.

      - These changes are very stable and do not change.

      - These changes cause the brain to overreact to drug- and alcohol-related cues.

      - Gene changes provide scientific evidence that alcoholics can never safely use any substance.

**Delta FosB transcription factor—a signaling protein that regulates gene expression—is amplified.

6. **Rewire the brain not to use: Recovery brain push-ups**

   - The human brain has one hundred billion neurons.

   - Each neuron has hundreds to thousands of connections.

   - You can unlearn/rewire powerfully built-in behaviors from substance abuse.

   - Rewiring is accomplished by the practice of new behaviors that are inconsistent with substance abuse and consistent with a program of recovery and therapeutic growth. The brain has the wonderful capability of making all kinds of new connections as a result of behaviors and what you do. It requires practice.

- Through practice, restore the brain's natural reward-reinforcement system to normal function.

- It can be enhanced though spiritual experiences, for example, as described by Bill Wilson and numerous others.

## D. Psychological factors

### 1. The "Addictive Personality"

- There is no one "alcoholic personality" or "drug-addict personality."

- There is the obsession with the alcohol or the drug and the compulsion to use. This may have something to do with changes in the brain, as well as psychological factors of reward that lead to addiction.

- Addicts and alcoholics use for all kinds of psychological reasons. What are yours?

a) Addiction is about being drawn to feeling good, then feeling even better. Good is not good enough.

b) A part of addiction can be the avoidance of emotional pain or the avoidance of emotional pain when you withdraw.

### 2. Psychological factors: Risk avoiders and risk takers. The whole idea about taking risks in recovery is to have a balance of risk taking and risk avoidance. Alcoholics and drug addicts who are using tend to be either on one side or the other of the spectrum in terms of taking risks.

- **Too much avoidance** of risk may be emotionally paralyzing; the fear of trying new things that might be helpful and good for you.

- **Too much risk taking** could put you in harm's way, especially if you say, "I'm going for it this one time and I can clean up again tomorrow," and this leads to a cascade of events that takes you to a full relapse that lasts for some unknown amount of time.

- **Risk avoiders and risk takers.**

a) Risk avoiders: introverted, find social situations difficult, may have emotional problems, tend to like downers and alcohol.

b) Nonalcoholics and non–drug addicts: tend to have more of a balance of risk taking and risk avoidance.

c) Risk takers: Extroverted, have higher energy, more socially engaged, tend to like alcohol and stimulants.

d) The more extroverted risk takers: impulsiveness might be a problem, sensation seeking, tend to like alcohol and stimulants.

- **Risk taking can work for you in recovery.** Risk trying all kinds of recovery behaviors, going to meetings, and meeting new people in recovery. Most of all, risk doing things and learn how to have fun without being loaded. If you don't learn how to have fun in recovery, you probably won't get sober.

3. **Psychological factors: stress and "soothability"**

- Get stressed, and your body goes into a "ready alert" (fight or flight) reaction to prepare for action. Hormones, like adrenaline, get dumped into your system.

- You relax after the response to stress, which is going back to baseline—being nonstressed. The ability to work with yourself and the things you do to help yourself to make the transition back from being stressed to being nonstressed is called "soothability."

- On average, addicts and alcoholics in recovery take longer than nonaddicts and nonalcoholics to get back to baseline after being stressed.

a) This is because the hormones associated with stress take longer to metabolize than for nonaddicts and nonalcoholics.

b) It may be caused by an overreaction to stress and having more of a response to recover from.

c) There may be more of a sensitivity to stress than nonaddicts or nonalcoholics.

- These are very good things to know about addicts and alcoholics in recovery. Learning and practicing how to deal with stress in non-substance-using ways may seem obvious, but it is a difficult thing to do. There are straightforward ways to handle it.

a) Stress buffers: Keep a good buffer between you and the point beyond your stress threshold that tips into feeling distressed. Predict stressors if you can, and manage what you are doing for the purpose of keeping in your buffer zone. Stress is part of life, particularly when unexpected things happen, but work on keeping yourself from going over your threshold to the distressed side.

b) Avoid looking for more stress if you are already stressed. A major ongoing goal of recovery is the opposite, which is to have and maintain a feeling of serenity.

c) In the recovery program, learn recovery mindfulness and meditation skills to increase your abilities at self-soothing.

## E. Cure versus management of addiction

- Chemical dependency is a chronic, irreversible, and progressive illness, and there is no cure.

- Any substance use is not safe and can trigger a reoccurrence of addictive use.

- Effective management of addictive illness through maintenance of sobriety is the measure of success in recovery.

## What contributes to the various parts of your addiction?

*Physical:*_____

_____

_____

_____

_____

_____

*Psychological:*_____

_____

_____

_____

_____

_____

*Social:*_____

_____

_____

_____

_____

# References

Alcoholics Anonymous (1952). *Twelve steps and twelve traditions.* New York: AA World Services

Brick, J. (2004). *Handbook of the medical consequences of alcohol and drug abuse.* New York: Haworth Press.

Cermak, T. (2006). *Recommendations to improve California's response to methamphetamine.* Position paper from the California Society of Addiction Medicine.

Condon, Timothy (2006). *Advances in drug abuse and addiction from NIDA: Implications for treatment.* In: California Society of Addiction Medicine: Addiction Review Course.

Elkhonon, G. (2001). *The executive brain: Frontal lobes and the civilized mind.* New York: Oxford University Press.

Goodwin, D.W., Schulsinger, F., Hermansen, L., Guze, S.B. & Winokur, G. (1973). *Alcohol problems in adoptees raised apart from biological parents.* Archives of General Psychiatry, 28, 238- 243.

Greene, R. (2000). *Supplementary scales, critical items and short forms.* In: The MMPI-2: An Interpretive Manual (2nd Ed.). Needham Heights, MA: Allyn & Bacon.

Kweek, M.J. & Koop, G.F. (1998). *Drug dependency: Stress and dysregulation of brain reward pathways.* Drug and Alcohol Dependency, 51, 23-47.

Kaij, L. (1960). *Alcoholism in twins.* Stockholm: Almqvist and Wiksell.

Kendler, K.S., Heath, A.C., Frayes, L.J., Neale, M.C. & Kessler, R.C., (1994). *A twin study of alcoholism in women.* American Journal of Psychiatry, 151 (5), 707-715.

McCausland, W.S. (1984). Unpublished doctoral dissertation, *Alcoholism treatment participation as a function of MMPI cluster type and life stress.* Ann Arbor: University Microfilms International.

Mooney, A. (1992). *The recovery book.* New York: Workman Publishing.

Nestler, E. (2001). *Molecular basis of long-term plasticity underlying addiction.* Neuroscience, Vol. 2, 119-128.

Pating, D. (2005). *Chemical dependency and psychiatric treatment.* Presentation to the Department of Psychiatry and Chemical Dependency, Kaiser Permanente, Santa Rosa.

Presti, D (2006). *The neurobiology of addiction.* In: California Society of Addiction Medicine: Addiction Review Course.

Presti, D. (2005). *The neurobology of addiction.* Presentation to the Department of Psychiatry and Chemical Dependency, Kaiser Permanente, Santa Rosa.

Rawson, R. (2006). *Treatment for methamphetamine-related disorders.* In: Meeting the Methamphetamine Challenge: Science, Clinical Care and Public Policy. San Francisco: CSAM Methamphetamine Conference.

Saxon, A. (2006). *Medical and psychiatric effects of methamphetamine abuse.* In: Meeting the Methamphetamine Challenge: Science, Clinical Care and Public Policy. San Francisco: CSAM Methamphetamine Conference.

Vieten, C. (2001). *Genetics of addiction: current topics in chemical dependency treatment.* Educational Symposium, Kaiser Permanente, Northern California.

Uhl, G. (2006). *The genetic basis for vulnerability to substance abuse.* In: California Society of Addiction Medicine: Addiction Review Course.

# SUCCESSFUL RECOVERY

## Stages of Recovery and
## Stages of Change

**Orientation. Stages of Recovery and Stages of Change.** This section describes the developmental process of recovery, motivation for change, and the relation to the Twelve Steps.

A. **Stages of Recovery:** Recovery develops over time, and there are significant events that characterize each stage.

- ✓ Still-using phase: Consequences of use cause you to begin bargaining strategies in an attempt to regain controlled use.

- ✓ Transition phase: Alcohol- or drug-related crisis, alibis exhausted, you seek help.

- ✓ Early recovery: Deal with a lot of adjustments to sobriety, learn about the disease of addiction, work on acceptance.

- ✓ Middle recovery: Work on resolving life's unfinished business and solidify recovery through self-analysis.

- ✓ Late recovery: Freedom through vigilance. Recovery becomes more integrated into who you are as a person; you develop a stronger sense of hope and purpose and help yourself by giving back.

B. **Stages of Change:** The change process and motivation.

- • Motivation can increase from being a user to a non-user.

- • Motivation can help move from one stage of recovery to the next.

- • There is personal resistance to change and also a process of going through it.

- • What is your readiness and confidence to make changes?

- • Stages of change:

  - ✓ **Precontemplation:** You don't recognize the problem, and there is no intention to change.

  - ✓ **Contemplation:** There is some awareness of the problem, and you see reasons to change and not to change.

  - ✓ **Preparation/determination:** You make a decision to change.

  - ✓ **Action:** You get help and make a commitment to a plan.

  - ✓ **Maintenance:** You continue the plan and work at solidifying it.

    <<<<<<<<<<<<<<<<<<<<<<<<<<<<>>>>>>>>>>>>>>>>>>>>>>>>>>>>>

    **Relapse:** occurs when the person falls out of recovery maintenance.

C. **Stages of Recovery and the Twelve Steps.** See how the stages of recovery and the Twelve Steps work.

A. **Stages of Recovery.** The process of recovery is something that develops over time, and there are milestones that are connected with each stage. It is a developmental process like a child that has to learn how to crawl before standing, has to learn standing before walking, has to learn walking before running, has to learn running before skipping. People watch their kids developing and sometimes check off the dates in a book when the child hits one of these developmental milestones.

In the same fashion as a human growing up, recovery tends to have fairly distinctive and observable phases. Your recovery develops as you move from one stage to the next. The following should give you a general idea of what to expect in each stage of recovery. The work that occurs in the phases of recovery (particularly the middle and late stages) is presented in an ideal sense. Know that the goal of recovery is progress, since it is always a work in progress and there is never an end state of perfection.

    1. **Still-Using Stage**

- To one degree or another, life revolves around using alcohol or drugs: preoccupation with the drug or alcohol, maintain the supply, substance-related lifestyle, and so on.

- Denial is automatic: Without thinking about it, the alcoholic or drug addict puts energy into the maintenance of denial. "There is a problem, but I don't really have it."

- Two pervasive beliefs:

  *First:* "I am not an alcoholic or a drug addict."

  *Second:* "I can control alcohol or drugs." (Of course, there would not be the need for the second belief if the first belief were really true.)

- Alcohol or drug-related consequences begin to shake the denial that covers the illusion about being in control.

- You begin various bargaining strategies in an attempt to regain control:

  ✓ **Let's slow it down:** "I'll use just as much, but I am not going to use so fast."

  ✓ **Let's not use as much:** "I'll cut down, but I am going to use as often."

  ✓ **Let's limit the time of day:** "I'm only going to use at . . ."

✓ **Let's control the number of days:** "I'm not going to use every day, just on . . ."

✓ **Let's try another substance:** "I have a problem with alcohol and I never had a problem with pot. I'll try some pot instead."

✓ **Let's add another substance:** "If I smoke a little pot, maybe I won't drink so much." "Maybe if I take a little Valium in the morning, I won't have such a hangover. (I can't drink in the morning, otherwise people will smell alcohol on my breath.)."

✓ **Let's treat the symptoms of substance abuse:** "I'm depressed. I better get some antidepressants." "I'm having problems with my partner. How about some couple's counseling?" "I need some work stress counseling."

✓ **Let's take a break:** "I'm going to stop using to get people off my back and to get back into control (but I am going to use again when the dust settles)."

- Bargaining strategies begin to not work over time, and the alcoholic or addict realizes on some level that there is an inability to control use.

2. **Transition Phase**

- An alcohol- or drug-related crisis creates motivation to be abstinent.

- The alibis, justifications, rationalizations, and other excuses for continued use become exhausted.

- You make a decision to do something about your addiction.

- The shift begins from using to not using.

- You move out of feeling and being isolated—locked into your own personal world of addiction—and you seek help.

- You detoxify from the alcohol or the drug and physical healing starts.

- The transition phase signals the beginning of the shift about beliefs concerning control.

- There is the beginning of a change in your core identity.

- You experience some relief with the decision to do something to help yourself.

3. **Early Recovery**

- Change one thing—don't use alcohol and drugs. Everything else in your life changes as a result. To a greater or lesser degree, the alcoholic or addict's life is wrapped around substance use, and stopping use creates a total reorganization of oneself. This causes a lot of adjustments, and even though you feel relief with the decision to stop using, there is stress caused by all of the changes.

- You learn about the disease of addiction, and this provides a way for understanding how your addiction evolved to get you where you are today.

- You develop a greater acceptance of not being in control.

- You take responsibility for your recovery, but at the same time you have the willingness and understanding for the need to rely on something outside yourself to get clean and sober.

- Stability develops through a continual repetition of new behaviors and practicing new beliefs.

- There is a shift in values to recovery-oriented meaning and purpose.

- You learn about non-drug-related ways of coping with life, problems, and stress.

- You begin to come to terms with the shame and guilt that is associated with substance abuse.

- You might feel a sense of euphoria about being in recovery, which is a honeymoon period that is called the "pink cloud."

4. **Middle Recovery**

- Some people call the beginning of middle recovery as "hitting the wall." The honeymoon is over, and you realize that you have many of the same problems even though you are sober. The recommendation is to have a "pink cloud parachute" by attending a lot of meetings, working with your sponsor, having a home group, doing step work, and having a support group.

- There is a lot of avoidance in the middle stage of recovery for many people, and as a result, there is some vulnerability for relapse. Hang in there.

- Middle recovery is starting to resolve your unfinished personal business though an emotional housecleaning.

- You solidify recovery though self-analysis.

- You examine of sources of conflict and anxiety.

- Dealing with resentments is a major issue for people in middle recovery.

- There is the beginning of addressing your personality problems that bother you or that get in your way.

- Restoring relationships starts, and wherever possible, you work on cleaning up damage you have done to others.

5. **Late Recovery**

- Here is the experience of what is called "freedom through vigilance." This means that you have a strong focus about recovery which gives you a sense of freedom.

- Recovery becomes more woven into the fabric of who you are, somewhat second nature, and more effortless.

- You apply the principles of recovery to everyday situations and see things through the lens of the fundamentals of recovery.

- You have daily conscious self-awareness and make self-corrections on the basis of that awareness (for example, becoming conscious of selfishness, dishonesty, resentment, and fear).

- You deal with "old tapes" (for example, the need for approval, past situations that remind you of defeat and humiliation, childhood abuses, and so on).

- Personal identity: "Who am I?" You might feel empty when you stop using alcohol and drugs because you don't know who you are.

    ✓ Using alcohol and drugs ties up a lot of time and is a distraction from developing a sense of oneself as a person. This is particularly true for people that started using during the critical personal identity development, the "Who am I?" years of life—the teens and early twenties.

✓   Defining yourself or addressing the identity issue can be scary because it could require you to take some emotional risks, have periods of confusion, and experience a sense of vulnerability. The process can also be exciting because you will find out things about yourself that you never knew before and you could feel more alive as a result.

✓   For example, you might start to make a stronger statement about who you are as a person by asking yourself the following questions: What do I really like and not like? Do the decisions I have made in the past really reflect what honestly works for me? What does "being true to myself" actually mean for me? What do I truly value? How do I define myself, what is my character, and what is my nature?

•   Late recovery is the development of stronger faith, inspiration, persistence, and feeling of hope and purpose.

•   Helping yourself by giving back: Help others who are in earlier phases of recovery helps your recovery. You reaffirm your recovery by helping others, and this keeps your recovery alive. It is a "mirror image process" because you see your addictive disease in others, and it is a reminder. The most important part is gifting your meaning of recovery is to others, and this generosity has a powerful effect for one's own recovery.

B.   **Stages of Change.** The stages of change relate to the levels of motivation and states of mind of changing from being a user to a non-user of drugs and alcohol. The stages of change identify one's process of intention and decision about continuing to use or not. The suffering chemically dependent person has to work with lowering resistance to change and denial and increasing insight in moving from one stage to another. You have to find your own way because feeling pressured from others might feel like criticism rather than offers of help. The stages of change define a motivational process.

1.   **Precontemplation.** At this stage, the chemically dependent person does not intend to change any behavior in the foreseeable future. Why? Because the person may be unaware or underaware of the existence of a problem. People around you may see a problem, but

you don't see it. Sometimes people who relapse revert back into being "precontemplators" and are in a tuned-out, unaware, or underaware mode. They start the stages of change over again.

2. **Contemplation.** To some degree, the chemically dependent person becomes aware of the problem, and this is usually caused by undeniable consequences of substance use. The person becomes ambivalent, that is, has uncertainty or indecisiveness about what to do. There are reasons to change and reasons to not to change. "I'm in a boatload of trouble and know something has to be different, but I like to get loaded and I don't want to change my (using) friends." The person is seriously thinking about changing, but there is no commitment yet.

3. **Preparation or Determination.** The person develops the intention to change and is getting ready to take some action. There may have already been a false start at sobriety, an attempt to stop or take action and then the return to use. Getting ready to quit is caused by an increase in psychological preparedness, and possibly though an increase of substance-related consequences. There is the actual decision to stop. You may stop right away, or it may take some time.

4. **Action.** You take action to change and to be abstinent and to overcome the problems related to it. You choose a strategy to change, get help, and make a commitment to a plan. There is the willingness to invest a considerable amount of time and energy into making changes for recovery.

5. **Maintenance.** You have chosen a way to get sober, and you stick to it. You consolidate the gains you have made along the way as work on a program of recovery. There is the awareness of relapse, and you create strategies and behaviors to prevent relapse. Of course, the goal of recovery is to stay in the maintenance stage.

6. **Relapse.** Relapse is falling out of the maintenance mode. It occurs though some form of complacency about maintaining recovery. There may be a stuck point in recovery, you get stalled, don't move through it, and regress.

**Motivation for Change.** Rate your readiness recovery and confidence about getting sober. Sometimes readiness and confidence about change shift depending on the day or your mood and may not be a constant thing. There also may be a discrepancy between how ready you are and how confident you feel. For example, you may be very ready, but you are not sure if you can get sober. The interaction of readiness and confidence is grist for the recovery mill. What can you do to enhance your readiness? What can you do to increase your confidence if you are ready, but your confidence is a little shaky?

## How Ready Are You?

1  2  3  4  5  6  7  8  9  10

**Not Ready**                                          **Ready**

*Rate yourself*

## How Confident Are You?

1  2  3  4  5  6  7  8  9  10

**Not Ready**                                          **Ready**

*Rate yourself*

Look for ways to enhance your motivation for actively maintaining your sobriety. For example, look for the payoffs—like feeling better emotionally, feeling better physically, being able to think more clearly, and feeling the other benefits of the healing process, such as new friends, restored relationships, looking better, making more money, freedom from fear, natural highs, and so on. You add to the list.

C.  **Stages of Recovery and the Twelve Steps.** The following is an application of the Twelve Steps to the stages of recovery and is an interpretation of the steps by the writer. Your sponsor may provide some different views of the steps as you work through them. Please refer to the AA Twelve Steps at the end of this chapter if you are unfamiliar with them, as well as the *Twelve Steps and Twelve Traditions* (published by Alcoholics Anonymous World Services Inc.).

Steps one through seven are the "personal steps" because they relate to the development of awareness of ourselves and our personal experience. Steps eight and nine are the "relationship steps" because they help you come to terms with unfinished business in relationships. Steps ten through twelve are the "ongoing recovery steps" since they increase your level of recovery with continued practice of being in the program.

- Steps 1–7:      The Personal Steps
- Steps 8–9:      The Relationship Steps
- Steps 10–12:      The Ongoing Recovery Steps

# Overview

**Early Recovery:**      **Step One** - Powerlessness and unmanageability

**Step Two** - Someone else can help you

**Step Three** - Allow someone to help

**Middle Recovery:**      **Step Four** - Knowing yourself

**Step Five** - Telling your story

**Step Six** - Defects of character

**Step Seven** - Defects of character and choices

**Step Eight** - Amends list

**Step Nine** - Making amends

**Late Recovery:**      **Step Ten** - Continued personal inventory and keeping emotionally current

**Step Eleven** - Conscious contact

Step Twelve - As a result of becoming more conscious, you are able to help others, thereby helping yourself. The integration of recovery principles into your life.

# Early Recovery:

1. **Step One.** A solid foundation is laid for step one: admitting and gaining full acceptance of powerlessness and life unmanageability related to the loss of control and use of alcohol or drugs. Step one is the foundation for recovery, regardless of whether you have one day or thirty years of sobriety. The punch line and paradox about recovery is that you have the beginnings of getting in control if you admit that you are out of control. Step one is the only one that you need to do perfectly; the others ask for progress, not perfection: "Only step one, where we made the 100 percent admission we were powerless over alcohol, can be practiced with absolute perfection. The remaining eleven steps state perfect ideals."

2. **Step Two.** You realize that your efforts to control alcohol or drugs basically do not work. You have hit some sort of personal bottom, and there isn't a cure for addiction, and seemingly there is no place to turn. Step two is about getting over one's personal defiance about being addicted and realizing there is the promise of hope for recovery.

"Came to believe that a Power greater than ourselves could return us to sanity" simply means that we take the next step after the acceptance of personal powerlessness and unmanageability and reach outside of ourselves to get help. We can't do it ourselves, and someone else has to help us recover.

The idea of "a Power greater than ourselves" seems simply too abstract for a lot of people, and for others, it is a point of resistance because of a fallacious connection to religion. For the purposes of recovery, you can make it very uncomplicated and concrete for yourself. "A Power greater than ourselves" is the clear truth about your addiction and knowing that everything else is some form of self-deception. The truth about your addiction can be based on pure science, a spiritual connection, help from others, the power of recovery groups, or a combination of many things.

Experiment with making your higher power a concrete concept: "A Power greater than ourselves" is the clear truth about your addiction and knowing that everything else is some form of self-deception.

"Could return us to sanity." This means nothing more than the reversal of the instability in your life caused by your addiction. It includes becoming reality-based and recovering from the reality distortions caused by the self-deception of addictive thinking.

3. **Step Three.** The third step is about willingness and having faith in someone outside ourselves to get sober. The main reason for this step is that self-will does not work. Having faith is not passive, but a process of actively investing yourself in something or someone to develop the confidence and trust that things will be okay: "turning it over." Increasing one's faith is central to recovery. Faith and willingness are interconnected and require the reduction of self-will and egotism.

One major personal development that occurs with step three is the cooperation with the program of recovery. The third step is coming to terms with your oppositions about being in recovery. You develop a partnership with your idea of a higher power.

Nearly everyone has faith to some degree. For example, joining the recovery program or a twelve-step group implies that you need help, you can't recover on your own, and you have faith that someone outside yourself will help you. You may realize that you are like a rudderless boat that needs guidance to be steered into safe harbor. Letting go and allowing yourself to be helped is having faith.

The concept of "turning it over" is difficult for alcoholics and drug addicts because it has a feeling of relinquishing control. Of course, in reality, you actually do not have anything to lose because you're not in control anyway! Turning it over is another one of those paradoxes of recovery. You get into control by relinquishing control.

You no longer have alcohol or drugs to kill your emotional pain, and what is one to do? Turning it over is having faith in the spiritual realm to help you or getting guidance and help from your recovery group, sponsor, and others who are truly helpful to your recovery. You no longer have to be isolated and locked up inside yourself because of the isolation that self-will causes.

The third step and turning it over takes you out of the self-punishing voices in your mind that say you are worthless and no good because you cannot control your addictive disease. It allows the storm of voices to calm down to a singular clear voice that is calming and that can bring you serenity.

Step three recommends that in times of conflict, indecision, and emotional disturbance, to rely on the Serenity Prayer: "God grant me the serenity to accept the things I cannot change, courage to change the things I can, and the wisdom to know the difference."

# Middle Recovery:

4. **Step Four.** Step four is a personal inventory and a guide to know yourself better. It is a beginning point for a lifetime practice of self-awareness and one major element of what it means to "be in recovery." It is called the "housecleaning step," but it is not a one-time event, since ongoing personal inventory is continued in the tenth step.

   Unlike steps one through three, where there is relief by letting go, the eventual relief provided by step four is by digging into yourself. The fourth step needs honesty, courage, and for you to provide an inventory without evasion of your past. Its goal is to work with the deception, lies, anger, resentments, pain, and guilt that have accumulated over time.

   Step four may automatically bring you closure on unresolved personal issues by the fact of just bringing them to light. One reason is that the process of writing the step brings clarity. The fifth step is meant to be a companion to the fourth step. The fifth is the telling of story that arises from completing your personal inventory.

   The fourth step is a rough survey related to how you feel secure and insecure within yourself as a person, how you may have caused damage to others and yourself in the pursuit of intimate relationships, and an inventory your resentments. Step four illuminates defects of character (see chapter 1 of the Successful Recovery portion of the workbook for examples of defects of character that might come up in working the steps). Your sponsor might suggest working your fourth step in four parts:

   1. Resentments

2. Fears

3. Sex conduct

4. Harm to others

Step Four: "Made a searching and fearless moral inventory of ourselves." A searching inventory means a realistic assessment of yourself. It is not meant to be an exercise in self-loathing or to give the critic within you free rein to judge or punish you.

The step about self-awareness, self-acceptance, and facing the secrets that make you emotionally sick. It works with your character flaws combined with chemical dependency. The housecleaning of the fourth step is aimed at unresolved feelings, unhealed memories, and character defects that have produced depression and loss of self-worth.

There is personal resistance and avoidance behavior in doing this step; that is why it requires you to be "fearless" and have courage in doing the step. A focus of the fourth step is to bring unconscious fears to light because they are the link to emotional insecurity and because fear is the "basic breeder of most human difficulties, the chief block to progress."

It is called a "moral inventory," not an "immoral inventory." It is a taking stock of good/bad aspects of your behavior and seeing how those behaviors may be in conflict with your values or the values you want to have. It is also called "moral" because you consider the effects of your behavior on others.

The step helps to untie one knot created by drinking and using drugs. There were the justifications, excuses of substance use. "We had made the invention of the alibis a fine art." There were conditions outside ourselves that gave the justification to continue using. What helped maintain the justification was self-righteousness, "vengeful resentments, self-pity, or unwarranted pride." The step says that harboring grudges ultimately results in beating ourselves with the club of anger that was meant for others. The fourth step reveals the importance of dropping blame from how we talk about others and from how we think. The step helps define how we need to take personal responsibility for our well-being.

The fourth step's one goal of making a resentment inventory is essential because resentment is the "number one offender" . . . "It destroys more alcoholics than anything else." The step gets at your hurts, how you have been abused, threatened, and what burns you up.

Your sponsor will give you guidance on how to do the fourth step, and the following will give an example and an idea of how the resentment portion of the step could be worked:

- I am resentful at: _____.

- The cause: _____.

- Affects my: _____.

> (examples: self-esteem, security, ambitions, personal relations, sex relations, etc.)

- Where I was to blame: _____.

Like the rest of the steps, the fourth is meant to be done with your sponsor for assistance on how to do it and, most of all, support for getting through it. The fourth step can bring up anxiety, guilt, anger, depression, etc. The step recommends extra professional help in addition to your sponsor if you need it.

The three characteristics of a good fourth step:

- ✓ First: Honesty. Having the courage to work with the past without evasion and face your fear in doing the step.

- ✓ Second: Thoroughness. Taking the time for self-examination. The process of writing itself provides clarity of what actually happened.

- ✓ Third: Balance. Focus on liabilities and defects, plus assets, strengths, and talents. Why? To have perspective.

5. **Step Five.** The fifth step is the "telling your story" step. It reveals the content of the fourth step. The fifth step is about coming to terms with your internal struggle, push to be honest through a sense of catharsis, and the release of pent-up feelings, which can feel cleansing. Its goal is to become more integrated and feel less fragmented. A feeling of fragmentation arises from the secrecy of your internal struggle, which also creates a sense of personal isolation. The nature of telling your story helps you feel less fragmented and more integrated and works at taking you out of a state of isolation.

The famous Swiss psychiatrist Carl Jung, who was instrumental in influencing the founding people of AA, said, "Telling our story is the beginning of our healing."

Your addictive disease has caused several things which the fifth step says to expect to feel better about:

- Rid yourself of terrible isolation

- Deal with feeling tortured by loneliness

- Resolve feeling that you don't quite belong

- Get over feeling like there is a mysterious barrier that exists between you and others that cannot either be surmounted or understood

- Helps you not feel like your life is akin to being an actor on a stage

Other things you should expect from the step is to feel a sense of inner healing and forgiveness, experience a new harmony, and experience some release from feelings of guilt. The step says that one reason it is difficult to do is because it requires "ego deflation." Admitting one's defects creates a sense of humility.

The step helps with having a more accurate self-assessment because most people find they are not exactly the monster they thought they were. Consequently, there is decreased anxiety because you will have a more reality-based perception of your shortcomings.

The twelve-step literature says that the fifth step is acknowledged as being the most difficult step and the one that is most necessary for long-term sobriety (and, of course, not forgetting the first step).

Revealing oneself in the fifth step is difficult for everyone. The distinguished psychologist Carl Rogers gives us some perspective: "What is often considered the most personal is the most universal. You are not the original 'great sinner.'"

Who do you take your fifth step with? The twelve-step literature has several suggestions. The person needs to have attributes that will create a positive experience for you. The person needs to be someone you can confide in and who will keep your confidence. There needs to be an understanding of the nature of the fifth step, as well as maturity and wisdom based on experience. It should also be done with someone who has been able to surmount serious difficulties. Additionally, you need to feel trust and compassion from the person. Examples of those with whom you can do the step: your sponsor, someone in the clergy, a psychologist, a therapist, a friend, etc. Some people have even gotten help from a stranger.

6. **Step Six.** Steps four and five cause steps six and seven to happen: The willingness to be ready to overcome personal shortcomings.

This step is the quintessential "progress, not perfection" step. What it asks is for the readiness for defects of character to be removed. Only step one requires 100 percent "perfection," that is, that you know and live the fact that you are powerless and your life is unmanageable in your relationship to alcohol and drugs. Step six is the attitude of beginning a lifetime's work on resolving defects of character. Step Six is the openness to personality change and the willingness to make changes as you navigate the path of recovery.

> Steps six and seven—the character defect steps—fully embrace the recovery concept of "progress, not perfection."

The fourth and fifth steps are difficult steps, and they tend to expose your defects of character. You may ask, "Now what?" You may think that something is missing because facing your personality issues is yet to be done. You might even feel an uneasiness or feel discouraged about your recovery program. The next step is actually coming to terms with defects of character.

The authors of the Twelve Steps were quite masterful in so many ways. Steps six and seven reflect the brilliance of the Twelve Steps, but in some ways, these two steps may seem fuzzy. Step six requires only a readiness to remove defects of character. Do they actually get removed? The answer is continue to be aware of defects of character, as well as to be ready to have them removed. The idea is to be aware of our personality flaws and work on improving them.

> Step six requires only a readiness to remove defects of character.

7. **Step Seven.** Steps six and seven are sometimes called the "forgotten steps." Some people gloss over them as though they don't exist or possibly do not realize the depth of the steps.

Step six and seven reveal the ingrained quality of defects of character and how challenging it is when thinking about making changes in your personality. Consequently, the sense of powerlessness that you experienced in the first step is revisited in the sixth and seventh steps, but in a different way. In relative comparison, the first step can be made like making a sharp U-turn in a speedboat. But the sixth and seventh steps are like making a very slow, gradual turn in an enormous barge.

You might find it helpful to think of this quote by George Bernard Shaw (1856–1950): "If you can't get rid of the skeleton in your closet, you'd best teach it to dance."

> If you can't rid yourself of the skeleton in your closet, you'd best teach it to dance.

Humility is the major factor of the seventh step. The step provides a spiritual solution by you humbly asking your higher power to remove your shortcomings. Humility is called for because this request is a tall order. We are also humbled by ourselves when we think about our shortcomings and how tough it is to make changes in defects of character. Think of humility when a defect of character reveals itself.

8. **Step Eight.** The eighth step is the relationship step. People are part of our past, and they are also part of our future. Unfinished business from the past tends to contaminate future relationships unless you come to terms with it. Unfinished business traps us in the past and robs us of being fully in the present

The eighth step is another inventory; it is an inventory of people that you have harmed. The second part of the step is developing the willingness to make amends to others and sometimes institutions. The ninth step is a companion step and is actually making the amends.

Step eight's goal is to make progress in having harmony with others. The eighth is a preparation step for making changes in your relationships and helping you be more honest and humble with others.

Of course, there is the personal payoff for getting resolution with others; for example, overcoming guilt, shame, remorse, interpersonal fear, resentment, low self-worth, etc. The ultimate is forgiving ourselves when we come to terms with others. You might also might find yourself putting your own name on your amends list!

> Put yourself on your amends list!

The technical aspect of this step is simple and easy, but the doing it is difficult. The suggestion is to not procrastinate. You might try sitting down for twenty minutes, do free flow, and write down everyone you can think of whom you have harmed. See what happens, and this is a start. Your sponsor will probably give you a lot of guidance.

An opinion: Please consider going beyond what is typically called for in step 8, and in the spirit of the recovery slogan, "accentuate the positive." Part of having harmony in relationships is acknowledging people who have guided you and have given you a helping hand. Consider doing an appreciations list of the people whom you want to thank, and directly thank them whenever possible.

9. **Step Nine.** The "making amends" step: "Made direct amends to such people wherever possible, except when to do so would injure them or others."

Step nine is another step that is often fought with avoidance because it requires you to come into contact with conflict that you have to resolve. Consequences of the disease of addiction tend to be the major grist for the mill in this step. Other than addiction-related consequences, it could cause us to be humble again since it most probably will point out some personal flaw.

Doing step nine does not guarantee peace of mind in others, approval of you, or another's acceptance or forgiveness of you. Like step three, you have to let go because you can't control the reaction of others, but in most cases, there will probably be a positive response to your amends.

What types of amends are there? Typically, amends fall in one of three categories:

- First is the material world or business amends. These have to do with any kind of negotiation that has been compromised because of mismanagement as a result of using alcohol or drugs. These relate to a gap in judgment, dishonesty, or some sort of avoidance of taking care of business. These could also have to do with money that you spent on yourself that should have been spent for other purposes, or money you have blown by trying to buy friendship or love.

- Second is the interpersonal amends. These are any kind of behavior that you feel bad about in your relationships, such as when you have been a bad example for your children. This area of amends can be very painful to deal with because you have to come to terms with your transgressions with those around you, abuses, and broken promises. Violations of trust fall in this category.

- Third is the area that relates to omissions. The omissions are the obligations that were neglected with respect to family, friends, work, your community, and yourself. This area has to do with not being present for others.

"Make a direct amends." Being direct is more powerful than being indirect. Being direct requires more courage, honesty, and humility. Being indirect is tainted with avoidance. Being direct is more respectful and more powerful from the standpoint of being better able to gain your self-respect.

"Whenever possible." Sometimes it is not possible to make direct amends because we have lost contact with certain people, or they have died, and so on. In these situations, you have to make an indirect amends. For example, you can make a charitable contribution, help someone else as a symbolic gesture, pray for someone, etc. Again, count on guidance from others in this area.

"Except when to do so would injure them or others." Step nine is neither masochistic nor sadistic. You do not want to hurt yourself or others. Examples would be an affair, something illegal, or another situation that could result in a devastating consequence if you were to make direct amends. This is an area that requires a very sensitive review with your sponsor and possibly others. This carefulness is part of why this step is later in recovery and requires a lot of thought and checking in with others.

# Late Recovery

10. **Step Ten.** This is the "freedom through vigilance" step. "Continued to take personal inventory and when we were wrong promptly admitted it." One reason for the step is that "emotional 'dry benders' often led straight to the bottle." This step takes a lot of practice, and the idea is that this step will eventually become automatic.

The tenth step is developing the habit of accurate self-appraisal. The step says it's a way of not accumulating any further unfinished emotional business and avoiding "emotional hangovers." One goal of the step is to work on living serenely though self-correction in the now.

The tenth step says that steps one through nine "prepare ourselves for the adventure of a new life," whereas step ten is the daily application of recovery principles "in fair weather or foul."

This step calls for the "acid test." Can you stay sober, keep emotional balance, and have an application of recovery principles under all conditions? The step is about continuous self-evaluation and inventory of personal assets and liabilities for the purpose of continual personal growth.

The tenth step is a daily visit with steps four and nine, which have to do with inventory and restitution. The difference is that step ten is done promptly in real time—it is about the present and doing personal spot checks. The operational basics of the tenth step are the continued watch for negative emotions, fear, anger, insecurity, selfishness, resentments, and dishonesty with yourself and in your relationships with others before they grow bigger.

It is also an interpersonal step because it looks at the way you react to others and treat them in daily situations. Doing it means letting go of resentment, anger, and brooding over injustices. The idea is to allow serenity and to have equanimity through promptly resolving unexpected disagreements and misunderstandings.

The step asks for you to become masterful at differentiating "stuffing" feelings versus practicing self-restraint. Knowing the difference requires being less impulsive and having better judgment. With practice, self-restraint becomes more automatic and equates to doing the right thing, rather than stuffing feelings or acting impulsively.

A direct quote of the tenth step: "In all these situations we need self-restraint, honest analysis of what is involved, a willingness to admit when the fault is ours, and an equal willingness to forgive when the fault is elsewhere. We need to not be discouraged when we fall into the error of our old ways, for these disciplines are not easy. We shall look for progress, not perfection."

You will notice personal patterns or "old tapes" when you practice the tenth step on a daily basis. Here are a number of examples negative tapes:

- The need to prove yourself

- Remembering defeat or humiliation that is still a sensitive area for you

- Fear and sensitivity about rejection

- Fear of abandonment

- The need for approval

- Insecurity

- Negative attitudes toward authority

- Harboring grudges and anger and dealing with those indirectly or being passive-aggressive

- The need to be on top

- Being selfish, arrogant, and devaluing other people

- Resentment and righteous anger

- Being overly vulnerable to allowing others to control your mood

- Catastrophic thinking or living in the future and attaching fear to it

- Ruminating about the past and being depressed

- Running shame, guilt, and remorse tapes in your mind.

- Having "should thoughts," which is operating on what you think you *should* do rather than what is ultimately the best thing for you.

- Automatically acting like your parents, especially with your own kids, rather than being in ways that are the best for you and others, and so on.

---

Who wouldn't want to get rid of these negative tapes?

---

Step ten is a daily operational version of step five, which is admitting shortcomings and, if needed, talking with a trusted person about the issues that you are grappling with.

Avoidance vs. readiness: Step 10 helps you revisit steps four through nine. There may be something in the past that is bothering you which remains unfinished. It may not necessarily mean that you are avoiding it because in reality, you may not be ready to tackle it. You may need more time and strength in recovery. Part of recovery is the self-assessment of avoidance versus readiness to get resolution.

Another upshot of the tenth step is a sense of courtesy, kindness, and a feeling of justice that brings oneself into harmony. The step says that the goal is to have the emotional balance sheet look pretty good at the end of the day—one day at a time!

11. **Step Eleven.** The second of the maintenance steps, the eleventh step seeks conscious contact through prayer and meditation. One basic premise of the step is to practice steps two and three on a daily basis.

This step is easy for some and hard for others because it requires a personal and spiritual conceptualization of a God consciousness, a higher power. The eleventh sounds rather mystical, but in actuality, it is a very practical step because it provides an emotional center that helps you negotiate everyday life. The step calls food the nourishment for the body and spirituality the nourishment for the soul.

Voltaire (1694–1778) puts a twist into the understanding of a God consciousness: "God is a comedian playing to an audience too afraid to laugh."

The step is difficult for some because of the Judeo-Christian-sounding overlay. It could be emotionally charged because of experiences in childhood upbringing and may be tainted through misunderstandings about the true nature of spirituality. Ill-fitting religious dogma of one's past experience has made the eleventh step a challenge for many working the twelve-step program. You might find it helpful to think of the AA tradition two, which says the ultimate authority is a loving god that is expressed through the group conscience of the twelve-step program.

Carl Jung, MD, whose influence was felt by the originators of AA, referred to a part of one's unconscious as the "collective unconscious," which is common to all people. Here, he applies the concept to a God consciousness.

- It arises in each person from shared inborn intuitive powers and universal experiences that all humans share in common and which are seen in all cultures.

- It is natural process of generalization in the human mind that combines common traits and experiences into a mostly identical basis for everyone's unconscious mind.

- A God or spiritual consciousness is revealed regardless of religion or culture, and it arises regardless of one's upbringing. It is animated by a willingness and an openness to experience it.

The eleventh step says there is a linkage between self-examination and prayer and meditation: "logically related and interwoven," and "the result is an unshakable foundation." The step provides more perspective: "remember that meditation is in reality intensely practical. One of its first fruits is emotional balance."

The step suggests that to maintain emotional balance, you can remember a particular prayer or phrase that will help you meditate: "Just saying it over and over will often enable us to clear a channel choked up with anger, fear, frustration, and misunderstanding."

A basic meditation practice is to sit in a chair with each vertebra in your spinal column more or less stacked vertically. Have your feet flat on the floor and your hands resting on your thighs. You may cast your eyes somewhat downward. Start to focus the meditation on each breath that you take, each inhalation and exhalation. Notice the drifting of your focus, thoughts that come up that distract you, or sounds that distract you. Then refocus your attention back on your breath. It is important in meditation not to judge or criticize yourself for loss of attention, but to just observe it and then to focus back on your breath and continue.

The idea expressed in the step is that prayer and meditation helps to gain strength and wisdom beyond one's usual capability: "And they [people in recovery] have increasingly found a peace of mind which can stand firm in the face of difficult circumstances."

12. **Step Twelve.** The steps mentions a "spiritual awakening," helping others in recovery, and "to practice these principles in all our affairs." The step asks the question, "A spiritual awakening, what is that?" The answer is that there are as many types of spiritual awakenings as people who have them.

The twelfth step says that a spiritual awakening is being gifted with a new consciousness and being. You are able to do, feel, and believe in ways that keep you clean and sober through practicing the principles of the twelve-step program. A spiritual awakening provides you easier access to a quiet place within yourself that speaks an inner truth for you.

Bill W., the cofounder of AA, related his dramatic experience of a spiritual awakening where there was the destruction of self-centeredness and he allowed a spiritual consciousness:

*These were revolutionary and drastic proposals, but the moment I fully accepted them, the effect was electric. There was a sense of victory, followed by a sense of serenity as I had never known. There was utter confidence. I felt lifted up, as though the great clean wind of a mountain top blew through and through. God comes to most men gradually, but the impact on me was sudden and profound.*

This famous quote from the Big Book of AA is quite striking, and we have to thank Bill W. for including the idea that it "comes to most men gradually" because we would not want to create any great expectations about a dramatic spiritual awakening. What you should expect is that a spiritual awakening happens over time and is an ongoing process which is unique to each individual.

A spiritual awakening usually follows a long period of emotional darkness and constriction, with an accompanying feeling of aloneness or isolation, or of being misunderstood. When one has an awakening, it feels deep. There is a sense of letting go and seeing things realistically as never before. There is a sense of empowerment. A spiritual awakening may have moments of tremendous insight where you feel more connected.

One way of viewing "carrying the message" is "giving it away to keep it." One of the most noted parts of doing the twelfth step is helping others who are suffering from chemical dependency. One purpose is to strengthen your recovery and continue personal growth by helping another person who suffers from chemical dependency. Sponsoring someone else who is at an earlier stage of recovery helps you get new insights about the steps and to see different dimensions of yourself as a recovering person. This step is a mentor-apprentice relationship for the sponsee to master basic skills.

The "mirror image process," where you see your own addictive thinking and behavior in someone else, is a major part of this step. This mirroring helps you objectively look at addiction in someone else and say to yourself, "I don't have to go there. I don't have to do that."

The reduction of egotism can result from giving to others. This is called altruism, or the unselfish concern and finding purpose by helping others. This help takes many forms, and the most obvious is being a sponsor. Other examples are doing service work, having a twelve-step meeting in a hospital or institution, working at the AA bookstore, manning the hotline, being a secretary at a meeting, doing a "twelve-step call," which is visiting a suffering chemically dependent person who needs help, and so on.

There has been some level of integration of the twelve-step program by the time you come to the twelfth step. There is a further integration in working the twelfth step: "practice these principles in all our affairs." "These principles" relate to the Twelve Steps, and "all our affairs" comprise the elements of our daily lives. The step is meant to be a summation and application of all previous steps.

# THE TWELVE STEPS OF AA

### Step One

*We admitted we were powerless over alcohol—that our lives had become unmanageable.*

### Step Two

*Came to believe that a Power greater than ourselves could restore us to sanity.*

### Step Three

*Made a decision to turn our will and our lives over to the care of God* as we understood Him.

### Step Four

*Made a searching and fearless moral inventory of ourselves.*

### Step Five

*Admitted to God, to ourselves, and to another human being the exact nature of our wrongs.*

### Step Six

*Were entirely ready to have God remove all these defects of character.*

### Step Seven

*Humbly asked Him to remove our shortcomings.*

### Step Eight

*Made a list of all persons we had harmed, and became willing to make amends to them all.*

### Step Nine

*Made direct amends to such people, wherever possible, except when to do so would injure them or others.*

### Step Ten

*Continued to take personal inventory and when we were wrong promptly admitted it.*

### Step Eleven

*Sought through prayer and meditation to improve our conscious contact with God as we understood Him, praying only for knowledge of His will for us and the power to carry that out.*

### Step Twelve

*Having had a spiritual awakening as the result of these steps, we tried to carry this message to alcoholics, and practice these principles in all our affairs.*

# References

Alcoholics Anonymous (1976). *Alcoholics anonymous (Third Ed.).* New York: AA World Services.

Alcoholics Anonymous (2001). *Alcoholics anonymous (Fourth Ed.).* New York: AA World Services.

Alcoholics Anonymous (1976). *Living sober.* New York: AA World Services.

Alcoholics Anonymous (1952). *Twelve steps and twelve traditions.* New York: AA World Services.

Brown, C. (1985). *Treating the alcoholic: A developmental model of recovery.* New York: Wiley & Sons.

Brown, C. (1992-2000). *The developmental model of recovery.* Annual consultation group, Asilomar, California.

Goldman, M. (1995). *Treatment II: Planning and implementation.* In: The assessment and treatment of psychoactive use disorders. S. Brown and R. Hester (Eds.). Conference materials from the University of California, San Diego for certification APA College of Professional Psychology.

Hazelden Foundation (1993). *The twelve steps of alcoholics anonymous: Interpreted by the Hazelden Foundation.* Center City, Minnesota: Hazelden.

McCausland, W.S. (1984). Unpublished doctoral dissertation, *Alcoholism treatment participation as a function of MMPI cluster type and life stress*. Ann Arbor: University Microfilms International.

Prochaska, J. & DiClemente, C. (1986). *Toward a comprehensive model of change*. In: W.R. Miller & N. Heather (Eds.), Treating addictive behaviors: Process of change. New York: Plenum Press.

# SUCCESSFUL RECOVERY

### Understanding Powerlessness
### and Unmanageability

---

**Orientation.** The purpose of this chapter is to start or contribute to an in-depth understanding of powerlessness and unmanageability. Understanding the concepts of powerlessness and unmanageability are pivotal for either succeeding in recovery or relapsing. You will relapse if this understanding fades in your conscious awareness. The chapter contains exercises that are heavily influenced by step one of the Twelve Steps, but in no way are they meant to substitute for working step one with your sponsor.

    A.   **Perspective.** No one had the intention to become addicted.

    B.   **The black box syndrome.** The final common pathway is that you are addicted no matter what the elements were that led to your addiction.

    C.   **Foundation for recovery:** *Acceptance* of powerlessness and unmanageability. Acceptance does not mean you have to like it.

    D.   **Concepts.** Powerlessness is over the alcohol or drug itself. Unmanageability reflects the consequences of use.

    E.   **Distortions in early recovery.** Looking for ways to use alcohol or drugs again.

    F.   **Minimizing powerlessness and unmanageability.** Leads to rationalizations which justify eventual use of alcohol or drugs.

    G.   **Attempts at controlled use.** Bargaining with the addiction in an attempt to be in control.

    H.   **Personal unmanageability.** The consequences of alcohol or drug use on you.

    I.   **Social unmanageability.** The consequences of alcohol or drug use on others.

---

**A.**   **Perspective.** No one had the intention to become an alcoholic or a drug addict when substance use began. What happened?

    •   There were problems with control or an inability to predict control.

- There was continued use despite negative consequences.

- There was compulsiveness around the use of alcohol or drugs.

- There was unconscious self-deception: "My disease tells me I don't have a disease."

B. **The Black Box Syndrome and the Final Common Pathway of Addiction.** There are many factors that add input to the inner workings that create your addiction to alcohol or drugs. Despite all of the contributing factors, the most important concern in recovery is the final common pathway: realizing powerlessness and unmanageability over the use of alcohol or drugs.

- There are many reasons why chemical dependency exists, and the reasons are different for each person. The results are similar.

- Response to mood-altering chemicals with a superphysical effect

- Allows you to develop psychological dependency

- You are not necessarily responsible having addiction.

- You are responsible for understanding the disease of addiction and for recovery.

- You are responsible for accepting powerlessness and unmanageability.

- Identifying powerlessness and unmanageability may involve a certain amount of emotional pain since you have to look at being out of control and the consequences.

This famous quote from the Big Book should shed some light on the pain that ultimately leads to acceptance. The Big Book discusses acceptance of addiction, conceding to your innermost self the reality of being addicted, and acceptance being the first step to recovery. Despite attempts at use, no real addict or alcoholic regains control once it is lost: "All of us felt at times that we were regaining control, but such intervals—usually brief—were inevitably followed by still less control, which led in time to pitiful and incomprehensible demoralization."

C. **Foundations for Recovery**

- Acceptance of powerlessness and unmanageability is the foundation of recovery. For people new to sobriety and for old-timers alike . . . doing it one day at a time.

- In-depth understanding and acceptance of powerlessness and unmanageability

- Powerlessness: Problems with control over substance use.

- Unmanageability: The areas of your life that are negatively affected by substance use.

- *Acceptance* of powerlessness and unmanageability *does not mean that you have to like it!*

- Humility is the essence of acceptance.

- The *Twelve Steps and Twelve Traditions* say alcoholism is a "mental obsession and physical allergy," and the alcoholic or addict is driven by an obsession that is beyond control: "we were the victims of a mental obsession so mentally powerful that no amount of human willpower could break it."

- Forget or minimize powerlessness and unmanageability = eventual relapse

**D. Concepts for understanding powerlessness and unmanageability: Amount you used, the results of use, and whether the results of use were unacceptable.** Read each line horizontally:

- **First line:** *Not powerless or unmanageable.* Not having problems with control and consequently there are no bad results, so substance use is not a problem. Your use is acceptable to you. You keep on using.

- **Second line:** *Powerless but not unmanageable.* There is loss of control over your use, but you are able to avoid, manipulate, minimize, or deny the results of your use. Your use may still be acceptable to you. You may keep on using.

- **Third line:** *Powerless and unmanageable.* You admit powerlessness, as well as not being able to control the results of use. Use becomes unacceptable. You stop using.

| *Concept 1* | *Concept 2* | *Concept 3* |
|---|---|---|
| **In control or powerless over the** amount **I used** | **Able to avoid or powerless over the bad results of use** | **These results were acceptable or unacceptable** |
| If I could be a controlled user . . . | there wouldn't be any bad effects . . . | No problem |

| But I have tried over and over to control, and I have been unsuccessful. I'm powerless as a result of not being in control . . . | but if I avoid the *bad results* which come when I use . . . | No problem |
|---|---|---|
| Now I know that I can't control and I am *powerless*. | I tried over and over to control *results—unsuccessfully* . . . | As a result, my life is *unmanageable* or unacceptable to me. |

### E.  Common Distortions in Early Recovery

- "If I can discover the problems areas of my life, I'll be okay (job, mate, etc.)."

- "All I have to do is understand myself (why I let things bother me) and my addiction will be controlled."

- "My mate is too demanding, too critical; the family doesn't understand me."

### F.  Forget or Minimize Powerlessness and Unmanageability

**On the way to a relapse, I rationalize:**

- "I can have just one . . ." (Wrong.)

- "I am smart enough now (learned enough about addiction) that I can now avoid the harmful results which come with my use." (Wrong.)

- "My life wasn't that bad." (Wrong.)

### G.  Attempts at Controlled Use. Attempts at control actually imply that in reality you are out of control. The net effect of attempts at control is the realization that you are out of control.

- Slow down, same amount
- Not use as much
- Limit time of day
- Limit number of days
- Use another substance
- Switch type (beer instead of spirits)

- Take an additional drug in an attempt to cut down drug of choice
- Treat symptoms of use (depression, job stress, relationship problems, etc.)
- Take a break, but go back to use after a using crisis is over.

H. **Examples of Personal Unmanageability.** Personal unmanageability is the impact and consequences of your alcohol or drug use on you.

- Put yourself in danger
- Health problems
- Don't feel loved
- Self-centeredness
- Immaturity
- Don't feel worthwhile

- Self-esteem issues
- Self-respect issues
- Self-image issues
- Hospitalized
- Depressed
- Feeling suicidal

I. **Examples of Social Unmanageability.** Social unmanageability is the impact and consequences of your alcohol or drug use on others in relationship to you.

- Put others in danger
- Family arguments
- Fighting with others
- Lost jobs/promotions

- Shirked responsibilities
- Abusiveness to others
- DUI or other arrests
- Hurt and lost relationships/ friendships

**Workbook for Powerlessness and Unmanageability.** Complete the following sections to help you define powerlessness and unmanageability in relation to your substance use.

# POWERLESSNESS

1. Attempts at bargaining with the disease of addiction: How have you attempted to control your use of alcohol or drugs? (Examples: limit amount, time of day, days of week, switch substances, etc.)

a. _____ *NO* _____

b. _____

c. _____

d. _____

e. _____

2. What have been the results of failed attempts at control? (Examples: anxiety and fear, depression, hopelessness, feeling like a failure, desperation, guilt, shame, sinking deeper into denial, such as rationalizing or justifying use.)

a. _____

b. _____ Guilt, Self _____

c. _____ loathing _____

d. _____

e. _____

3. What convinces you that you cannot safely use alcohol or drugs?

Health &
Safety
my family
my family his start

## PERSONAL UNMANAGEABILITY

1. How have you put yourself in danger because of your use of alcohol or drugs?

DUJ x2

2. What is the effect of substance use on your personal health?

w t 6ah
Nocturi'
& else

3. What has been your need for professional help which was directly or indirectly due to your use of alcohol or drugs (medical help, need for emergency care, hospitalization, psychiatric care, psychiatric hospitalization, etc.)?

*No need?*

4. What has been your emotional unmanageability which resulted from substance use (depression, anxiety, fear, emotional instability, suicidal feelings, etc.)?

*mild answer*

5. What have been the personal characteristics that reflect unmanageability? (Examples: self-centeredness, immaturity, self-esteem problems, and poor self-image.)

6. How have you lost self-respect because of your use of alcohol or drugs?

*?*

# SOCIAL UNMANAGEABILITY

1. How have you put others in danger because of your use of alcohol or drugs?

*2 pairs*

2. What conflicts with others and relationship issues were directly or indirectly caused by your use of alcohol or drugs? (Examples: family arguments, fighting with others, abusiveness, conflicts due to financial loss.)

a. _____
b. _____ *∅ I can think of*
c. _____
d. _____
e. _____

3. What alcohol- or drug-related behaviors have your family and friends had a problem with?

a. _____ *Father, brother*
b. _____ *Paternal uncles*
c. _____
d. _____
e. _____

4. What has been the impact on your functioning (lost jobs/promotions, missing school, not getting ahead, work stress, shirked responsibilities, manipulating to cover yourself at work, etc.)?

a. _____ *I have been a high*
b. _____ *functioning Crank*
c. _____
d. _____
e. _____

5. Have there been arrests and other legal problems directly or indirectly related to alcohol or drugs (such as DUI)?

*DUI*
*x2*

# ADMITTING VS. ACCEPTING POWERLESSNESS AND UNMANAGEABILITY

1. What is the difference between admitting and accepting powerlessness and unmanageability?

*?*

2. Are you an alcoholic or drug addict?

*Binse of Alcoholic*

3. How are you admitting it or accepting it?

*Admit + Accept*

**4.** What are the compelling reasons for you to stay in a program of recovery?

a. _____ *Health, Job*

b. _____ *Family*

c. _____

d. _____

e. _____

f. _____

g. _____

h. _____

i. _____

j. _____

# References

Alcoholics Anonymous (1976). *Alcoholics anonymous (Third Ed.).* New York: AA World Services.

Alcoholics Anonymous (2001). *Alcoholics anonymous (Fourth Ed.).* New York: AA World Services.

Alcoholics Anonymous (1952). *Twelve steps and twelve traditions.* New York: AA World Services.

Brown, C. (1992-2000). *The developmental model of recovery.* Annual consultation group, Asilomar, California.

Hazelden Foundation (1993). *The twelve steps of alcoholics anonymous: Interpreted by the Hazelden Foundation.* Center City, Minnesota: Hazelden.

# Index

## A

abstinence, 3–4, 11, 16–17, 19, 53, 65, 67

acceptance, 2, 7–8, 37–39, 75, 84, 92, 102–4

addiction, 2–5, 10–11, 17, 20–21, 29, 31, 35, 37–39, 48–52, 63–66, 72–75, 77–78, 84–85, 102–3, 105–6

family disease of, 21, 48

management of, 63, 72

power of, 17, 65

sexual, 23

addictive illness, 5, 11–12, 19–20, 31, 38, 48, 65–66, 72

power of, 11–12

addicts, 5, 20, 35, 38, 48, 53, 64, 70–71, 77, 104

alcohol, 4–6, 8–9, 11–12, 17–23, 32–36, 40–42, 45–48, 50–52, 59–60, 64–65, 67–71, 75–78, 84–85, 102–3, 106–10

alcoholic families, 59, 66

alcoholics, 5, 12, 15, 29, 35–36, 43, 52, 56, 64, 69–71, 85, 87, 100, 111

Alcoholics Anonymous (AA), 17, 23, 29, 31–32, 43, 47–48, 50, 54, 56–57, 63, 73, 83, 96, 98–100, 111

Big Book of, 28, 38, 43–44, 103

Alcoholics Anonymous World Services Inc, 83

alcoholism, 38, 73–74, 104

alcoholism treatment participation, 56, 74, 101

allergy, physical, 63, 104

anger, 6, 21, 28, 39–40, 86–88, 94–95, 97

anxiety, 4, 7–8, 10, 21, 28, 41–42, 44, 65, 79, 88, 107–8

avoidance, 26, 28–29, 34, 53, 70, 79, 92–93, 95–96

## B

black box syndrome, 102–3

boredom, 8, 21, 42

## C

change, 1–4, 6, 8, 29–30, 32–34, 37, 40–41, 48–49, 68–70, 75, 77–78, 80–81, 86, 90–91, 101

gene, 69

progressive, 69

stages of, 80–81

chemical dependency, 64, 72, 74, 87, 98, 103

commitment, 12, 75, 81

complacency, 19, 28, 53–54, 81

compulsion, 1, 8–10, 31, 46, 63–64, 70

compulsive behaviors, 3, 28, 47, 49

confidence, 75, 81–82, 85, 89

conflicts, 20–21, 28, 35–36, 47, 49, 58, 79, 86–87, 92, 109

coping, 8, 18, 20–21, 40, 78

coping mechanisms, 3, 16, 19

## U

unmanageability, 2–3, 6, 83–84, 102–6, 108, 110

personal, 102, 106–7

social, 102, 106, 109

## V

Voltaire, 96

## W

warning signs, 2, 26, 29, 36, 46, 55

Wilson, Bill, 70, 98

withdrawal, 69

Printed in the United States
By Bookmasters